BUILD A DYNAMIC ORGANIZATIONAL CULTURE

"A 7-Step TEAM Approach"

Rod Jonas, Ph.D.

Copyright © 2024 ROD JONAS

All Rights Reserved. No part of this publication may be reproduced, distributed, or transmitted in any form or by any means—electronic, mechanical, photocopy, recording, or any other—except for brief quotations of the authors or editor.

Although the authors and editor have made every effort to ensure that the information in this book was correct at press time, the authors and editor do not assume and hereby disclaim any liability to any party for any loss, damage, or disruption caused by errors or omissions, whether such errors or omissions result from negligence, accident, or any other cause.

Endorsements

Dr. Rod Jonas has been making a profound impact on higher education for many years. A teacher and a coach at heart, Rod brings energetic leadership, an innovative spirit, and tenacious diligence to his work, made evident by his remarkable rapport with all who work with him. As our founding Dean of the Liffrig Family School of Education and Behavioral Sciences at the University of Mary since 2009, Rod has proved to be a vital resource for the development of curriculum, the support of faculty, and genuine care for students. Due in large part to Rod's wealth of experience and visionary guidance, the Liffrig Family School of Education and Behavioral Sciences has undergone tremendous growth, all the while successfully forming and preparing strong professionals who are bringing world-class academic experience and moral courage into their classrooms, clinics, and offices.

At a time when teachers, counselors, social workers, criminal justice professionals, and psychologists are facing tremendous challenges in a world which is battling turmoil, Rod has created an impressive culture within his school, instilling hope, and grit, and preparing students who will be working in those often difficult and tragic situations. Rod is a leader of integrity with keen insight and strong conviction - and how grateful we are for his generosity in sharing his talents and experience with us.

Monsignor James Shea, President, University of Mary

As the Executive Director of NDCEL (North Dakota Council of Educational Leaders), there is not a day that goes by where there is not a conversation that takes place about building positive culture and the importance of culture to have success in school or the workplace. Again and again, we recommend and rely on Dr. Rod Jonas as the expert in this area. He is highly sought after by school leaders based on his outstanding leadership and ability to build, create, and teach how to build a dynamic school culture and has a proven track record in doing so, as the Dean of the Liffrig Family School of Education and Behavioral Sciences at the University of Mary. Dr. Jonas was my first teacher in the field of education years ago, and his skills have led him to be undoubtedly one of the best collegiate deans and experts in the field of education.

Dr. Aimee Copas, Executive Director, North Dakota Council of Educational Leaders

Dr. Jonas is a dynamic and experienced leader at the University of Mary. He has developed a positive and vibrant school culture that empowers faculty and staff to take risks and be creative. He understands the importance of prioritizing advocacy for his school to provide them with the resources they need to help strengthen and improve their academic programs. Relationships are central to a high functioning organization. Dr. Jonas engages every faculty and staff member in his school at least once a week, so they know he is invested in them and the work they do. His priority on developing a dynamic organizational culture allows faculty to take the initiative to improve their academic programs. The results of his leadership are evident in the retention of excellent and dedicated faculty as well as outstanding graduates.

Dr. Diane Fladeland, Vice President Academic Affairs, University of Mary

Leadership can be defined as the art of mobilizing others to work together toward shared aspirations. This is not an easy task, but the development of the Liffrig School of Education and Behavioral Sciences under the leadership of Dr. Rod Jonas is a fine example of this leadership definition. Dr. Jonas clearly set and articulated the standards that set the path to success for the school. His vision of a vibrant, forward-looking Liffrig Family School of Education and Behavioral Sciences was soon shared with carefully chosen faculty and staff. By melding this vision with the University of Mary's mission and values and students who were excited to become a part of the Liffrig School of Education and Behavioral Sciences, a culture of professionalism and excellence was established.

Leadership and the creation of a shared vision is not an easy task, but Dr. Jonas willingly accepted the challenge. His honest and clearly articulated style of leadership is obvious to all who experience the school and inspires them to become part of its development and success. He is a talented and passionate leader who gives credit to the entire school team. When challenges are encountered, they are accepted by the members of the school as opportunities for growth. Fear of failure has no place in this culture. Staff members are hired with this growth and success philosophy in mind and then encouraged to use their gifts to help continue to grow the vision. As a result, the Liffrig Family School of Education and Behavioral Sciences has the respect of the University, community professionals, alumni, and donors.

Neal Kalberer, Former Vice President Public Affairs, University of Mary (retired)

Table of Contents

Introduction	12
Chapter 1: Step #1 – Before You Build Culture, Know What It Is You Are Trying to Build	18
Team Chemistry and Culture	20
Climate and Culture	24
Defining Organizational Culture	26
Building a Dynamic Organizational Culture in Education	28
University of Mary's Organizational Culture	31
Value of an Organization's Artifacts	34
Chapter 1 – Lessons Learned	37
Chapter 2: Step #2 – Develop a Leader-Leader Mindset	38
Learn to Lead by Leading	41
Servant Leadership	44
Transformational leadership	47
Leader-Leader Leadership Philosophy	48
Chapter 2 – Lessons Learned	51
Chapter 3: Step #3 – Build Your **TEAM**	52
Recruit and Hire People Who are a Great Fit	55
Recruit Great Teammates	59
Create a Recruiting Process and Philosophy	67
Create a Leadership Team	72
My Starting Five	77
Chapter 3 – Lessons Learned	81

Chapter 4: Step #4 – Develop Your **TEAM** Leadership Principles ... 82

    Define Your Team's Leadership Principles ... 83

        Do the right thing, even if it is hard to do ... 85

        Take the time to praise real effort and achievement ... 86

        Lead with patience and respect ... 88

        Let faculty make the decision for which they are responsible ... 91

        Lead selflessly – Think less of what is best for you and more about what is best best for our school, our faculty, and our students ... 93

        Deal with conflict – Get the truth on the table ... 94

    Bring Your Leadership Principles to Life ... 97

    Chapter 4 – Lessons Learned ... 99

Chapter 5: Step #5 – Create an Identity ... 100

    Organizational Values and Identity ... 101

    What Words Describe Who You Are ... 105

    Developing and Defining Your Identity ... 109

    Continue to Build Your Identity ... 117

    Chapter 5 – Lessons Learned ... 119

Chapter 6: Step #6 – Create a Shared-Governance Organizational Structure ... 120

    Impact of an Organizational Structure ... 120

    Higher Education Organizational Structure ... 123

    Our School's Organizational Structure ... 126

    Faculty Workload Assignments ... 130

Chapter 6 – Lessons Learned	134
Chapter 7: Step #7 – Avoid the "Manager Black Hole"	136
Leader-First Mindset	139
Are you a Leader or a Manager	140
Leaders Know Their Product	146
Chapter 7 – Lessons Learned	153
Chapter 8: Final Thoughts	154
Afterword	162
Acknowledgements	166
References – Chapter 1	170
References – Chapter 2	176
References – Chapter 3	180
References – Chapter 4	184
References – Chapter 5	188
References – Chapter 6	194
References – Chapter 7	198
References – Chapter 8	200

Introduction

My motivation for writing and the content in this book comes primarily from my experiences as a Dean at the University of Mary, a private Catholic university in Bismarck, North Dakota.

I have always been motivated to lead, but in my role as Dean, I was given the unique opportunity to build an academic school from the ground up.

For any organizational leader, the task of building an organizational culture is an important responsibility. As a leader, the quote I have read that resonates with me the most, is Edgar Schein's quote, *"The only thing of real importance that leaders do is create and manage culture. If you do not manage culture, it manages you, and you may not even be aware to the extent to which this is happening."*

Yet, when I talk to organizational leaders or give presentations on the importance of building an organizational culture, I am always surprised by the participants' lack of knowledge in this area and, even more, surprised by the lack of understanding of the benefits of having a strong and positive organizational culture.

Prior to 2009, the academic units at the University of Mary were organized as departments, with a chair assigned as the administrator for each department. In 2009, a new institutional organizational structure was created, and academic departments were reorganized into schools. I was hired as a Dean for one of the new schools, the Liffrig Family School of Education and Behavioral Sciences, which included undergraduate programs in education, social work, psychology and criminal justice and graduate programs in education and counseling.

In my role as Dean, I was given the authority, autonomy and resources needed to build our school as well as the unique opportunity to create what I termed a *dynamic* organizational culture, a culture where people are given the freedom to innovate and where change is embraced as the norm. I feel blessed to be given this opportunity and the authority to hire the faculty and staff needed to create a *dynamic* organizational culture that improved teamwork, collaboration, and faculty retention, but most importantly, improved our faculty and staff's willingness to take risks and innovate.

As I near retirement, it is important to tell the story of my leadership journey. It is a story I believe can help any organizational leader who is willing to allow their followers to lead, who wants to improve the effectiveness of their organization, and who is passionate about making a difference in the lives of those they lead.

My leadership principles and philosophy have evolved from my experiences as a teacher, coach, professor, and university administrator. I have been led by leaders with different leadership philosophies and styles, including autocratic leaders, democratic leaders, transactional leaders, transformational leaders, situational leaders, adaptive leaders, and servant leaders, but nothing has taught me more than leading alongside those I serve.

Simon Sinek, a British-American inspirational speaker, and author of five books, including *Start With Why* (2009) and *The Infinite Game* (2019), is fond of saying that being a leader means one thing only – "*it means you have followers.*" What I have learned from those who have chosen to follow me has made me the leader I am today. It has taught me the leadership lessons and the culture development strategies outlined in this book.

My leadership journey began in the early 1980s after reading *In Search of Excellence* by Peters and Waterman (1982). This classic management book investigated the qualities common to the best-run companies in America. I often saw this book on the desk of a successful NCAA football coach when I was a graduate assistant. One day, I asked him why he had this book on his desk, and he replied,

"I am trying to become a stronger leader and a better football coach, so I need to learn more about leading. This book is about how the best leaders lead. Here, you can have my copy. It might change your ideas about leadership."

I willingly accepted his offer, and that very night read the book cover to cover. It kickstarted my leadership journey, providing the impetus I needed to develop my own leadership philosophy. It also helped me begin to develop a better understanding of how to build a *dynamic* organizational culture and was a key first step in helping me develop my own leadership philosophy.

During the 1980s and until 1995, I coached at the high school and college levels. These coaching experiences were foundational in the development of my leadership philosophy and the leadership principles I would follow as a leader. As a coach, I learned that coaching is the ultimate leadership lab school because there is no better teacher than a scoreboard. No leader will become an effective leader until they have had their leadership principles tested and, more importantly, learned to fail and get kicked around a little.

As a coach, after every game, you are labeled a winner or a loser. Dealing with this reality either makes you a weaker leader or a stronger one. I have seen coaches succumb to the pressures of winning and thereby fail as leaders. I will never forget the leadership principles I learned as a coach by being on the hot seat.

My coaching career taught me the importance of grit and perseverance, but most of all, it taught me the importance of understanding the leadership principles needed to help others succeed and come together to build the culture needed to thrive as individuals and as a **TEAM**.

No leader can succeed if they do not know who they are and what they believe in. A leader's leadership beliefs and principles are what guide them during tough times and in times of change and uncertainty.

In the 1970s and 1980s, most coaches coached with an authoritarian and autocratic leadership style. There were exceptions, but most ruled with an iron fist and *'my way or the highway'* mentality.

Coach Mike Krzyzewski at Duke University was different, not only in his leadership style but the way his teams played. I personally attended some of his coaching clinics and even had one of his assistant coaches come to our campus to put on a clinic for basketball coaches in our state. I became a Dukie, followed the team religiously, and attended two of the Final Four games Duke participated in during late 1980s and early 1990s.

What struck me most about Coach Krzyzewski was how he led, managed, and developed his players. He looked at each player's strengths and tried to maximize their talents. He let players play and gave them the freedom to make decisions on the court. Most importantly, he let his players lead, not just follow. He expected each player to play a role, even those sitting on the bench. He built a team culture that brought out the best in everyone, with his teams built from the inside out.

A prime example of Coach Krzyzewski's leadership philosophy at work: after each dead ball, his team would huddle on the court and talk to each other. It was a novel strategy and something I had never seen from another coach. He expected his players to communicate on the court, to step up and take charge. This strategy is now emulated by every coach in America, but it all started with Coach Krzyzewski.

Coach Krzyzewski went on to author several books on leadership, but his first was *Leading with Heart* (2001), which became a New York Times bestseller. The book focused on successful leadership strategies he used as a coach. Coach Krzyzewski retired in 2022 but led the Blue Devils to five national titles, 13 Final Fours, 15 ACC tournament championships, and 13 ACC regular season titles. Coach

Krzyzewski also coached the United States national team and led them to three gold medals at the 2008, 2012, and 2016 Olympics. He is a two-time inductee into the Naismith Memorial Basketball Hall of Fame and is regarded as one of the all-time best college basketball coaches.

My decision to follow him, although from afar, turned out to be a wise one. I have read all his books, and there were always certain sections of each book or a certain phrase that resonated with me. One phrase I read that has stuck with me on my leadership journey is, *"Each team has to run its own race."* I have tried to remember this phrase as I built my basketball teams and today in the building of my school **TEAM** at the University of Mary. Every team I have worked with is unique, with special talents and gifts, and I have tried to remember to allow each team to chase its own dream and run its own race.

After leaving coaching and entering the world of higher education, I took the coaching leadership lessons I had learned and tried to put them into practice. Some of my leadership ideas worked, but others floundered because I was no longer leading college student-athletes but professionals with doctoral degrees who did not need to be told how to do things. I learned through trial and error that professionals needed to be inspired, not managed.

It was clear to me I was now leading people smarter than me, with expertise in areas I knew little about. So, once again, my leadership philosophy needed to evolve. As I moved into the world of higher education administration, I often stumbled and failed, but my leadership philosophy was being put to the test and transforming in ways I did not even realize. I was running a different race with my faculty than I was with my basketball players, and I needed faculty and staff members who were eager to run the race with me.

This book is about my leadership journey and the story of the steps I took to build our **TEAM** and create a *dynamic* organizational culture that has allowed our school to grow in student enrollment and the number of academic programs. The faculty members in our school are dedicated, passionate and committed professionals focused on creating and developing strong academic programs that meet the needs of our students. It has made our school a joyful place to work and a place where creativity and innovation thrive.

We are a **TEAM** running its own race, with every member playing a key role in our success. All I did as their leader was invite them on the journey and allow them to have the authority to lead to create their own futures as members of the team. We have, at times, been on a bumpy ride, but we have stayed the course and always believed that if we hired talented and committed people who trusted each other, we would succeed. So, this book is about this journey and how our school **TEAM** was able to create the *dynamic* organizational culture needed to allow our school to grow and flourish.

Chapter 1

Step 1 – Before You Build Culture, Know What It Is You Are Trying to Build

The only thing of real importance that leaders do is create and manage culture. If you do not manage culture, it manages you, and you may not even be aware of the extent to which this is happening."

- Edgar Schein

As I mentioned in my introduction, this quote is by Edgar Schein, a well-known and influential author in the field of organizational culture, whose book *Organizational Culture and Leadership* is one of the most comprehensive books ever written on the subject. In his book, Schein discusses contemporary research in the field of organizational culture and the critical role organizational leaders play in creating and building a strong, positive organizational culture.

In this quote, Schein clearly emphasizes that creating or building an organization's culture is the most important responsibility of any leader. And as he points out, if a leader fails to take the time to create and build culture, beware because it will be built anyway. Why? Because an organization's culture is much like a person's personality. A person's personality often goes unnoticed by others until they must interact with another person or together solve a problem.

In the same sense, an organization's culture can go unnoticed, but when the organization needs to solve a problem, it is an organization's culture that will directly impact its ability to solve the problem and help the organization continue to improve and grow. Why? Because an organization's culture will determine how problems are dealt with, and it helps set expectations for how people interact, work together and function as a team.

Another quote I use often is, "*Culture eats strategy for breakfast.*" This quote is attributed to the late Peter Drucker, an American management consultant, educator and one of the best-known writers on management theory and practice. Drucker did not imply by this quote that strategy is not important, but that a focus on building a strong positive organizational culture is a much surer way to increase organizational effectiveness than relying on an organization's strategic planning efforts.

Organizational leaders often use this quote to provide evidence of the value of building a strong organizational culture. Peter Drucker wrote more than twenty-five books on leadership, organizational behavior, management theory and the practice of management. Shortly before his death, *Business Week* celebrated him as '*the man who invented management.*' His work has been a major contributor in helping managers understand how corporations function, with most of his ideas about management theory still relevant today.

Most organizations understand the importance of strategic planning and making data-based decisions. In today's world, anyone in a leadership position in any organization has more than likely played a role in developing the organization's strategic plan. Drucker believed, however, that an organization's strategic planning will fail if the organization does not have a strong organizational culture. Why? Because it is people who make strategic plans come to life. Without people who are innovative, engaged and committed to each other and the organization's core values, even the best-developed and well-thought-out strategic plan will not have the impact needed to improve the organization's effectiveness.

Drucker's research on organizational culture focused on the world of business, but research on organizational culture has been a topic of research in other disciplines, as well, including psychology, sociology, anthropology, and education. However, the term *'culture'* is defined differently in other disciplines. This is primarily because organizational culture is a hard concept to define and understand because elements at the core of an organization's culture are intangible, such as an organization's beliefs, norms, values, assumptions, and attitudes. In addition, these intangible elements of an organization's culture are intertwined with the organization's structure, policies, goals, and processes.

Every organization's culture is unique because each organization has its own mission, vision, values and structure, and each organizational leader has their own understanding of culture based on their leadership philosophy and past leadership experiences. Nevertheless, most leaders would agree that an organization's culture plays a critical role in the success of the organization, but for most leaders, even the simple task of defining and building an organization's culture can become complex and overwhelming.

Team Chemistry and Culture

My first exposure to understanding the value of a strong, positive organizational culture was as a college basketball coach in the 1980s and 1990s. In the coaching world at that time, a team's culture was called *'team chemistry.'* Most coaches would agree that team chemistry was an essential element in building a winning team, but when I was a college basketball coach, I do not remember a single coach ever defining team chemistry or explaining how a coach could build it.

In my second year as a head men's college basketball coach, we played a team we had played before. I knew the coach well as both a friend and colleague. My team played a great game, and we won by more than 20 points. After the game, the coach of this team said to me, *"You are going to have a successful season because I can tell your team has great chemistry."*

I was proud he thought our team had good chemistry, but what was it he saw that made him think my team had good team chemistry. Did he think my team worked hard and enjoyed playing together? Or did he see that my players seemed to get along, liked each other or communicated well? I did not know; I just knew it was a positive thing when a coach told you your team had good chemistry.

The coach's analysis of my team was accurate. That year, we won a conference championship and made it to the regional NAIA tournament. But to this day, I wonder: Was it truly team chemistry that made my team successful? If so, how was it created? Did I create it unknowingly, or did my players create it? All I know is they were truly a team with great leaders and players who were fun to coach because of their love for the game.

As the season rolled on, they got better and better and closer and closer as a team. I do not remember doing anything special to build the team's chemistry; it just seemed to happen on its own. I will never know if our team chemistry was the reason for our success; there were other variables that could have affected my team's performance. The only thing I know for sure is that I will never forget that team and the special season we had together.

A few years ago, I made a phone call to one of the players from this team, who is now a teacher and a coach. He was dealing with health problems, so I was checking in to see how he was doing. During the phone call, we talked about his health and our families, but inevitably, our conversation turned to basketball and our championship season. He spoke about how special that year was for him. At one point, he said, "*I would love to go back in time and relive that season again. It was so much fun.*"

He said he loved his teammates and talked about how close they were as a team and the players on that team are to this day his best friends. He never once spoke about wins or losses, only about his teammates and the times they had together. I really enjoyed talking to him and hearing about the impact that team had on him. The conversation reiterated the value of good team chemistry, not only in winning but in building strong lifelong relationships.

During my coaching days, even though I knew team chemistry was important and that my teams with team chemistry were more successful and more enjoyable to coach, I never really knew how to create it or purposely set out to create it. Also, as an assistant coach, I do not recall ever having a head coach discuss with me how he planned to create team chemistry.

At coaching clinics, basketball coaches would talk freely about their offensive or defensive systems and their practice drills, but I never heard any coach, even national championship coaches, ever talk about team chemistry, much less how to create it. It is as if teams either had good team chemistry or not with coaches having little influence.

Fast forward to today and the college and professional coaching world, and you will hear coaches talk freely about the importance of building a strong, positive team culture. The word *'chemistry'* has been replaced by *'culture,'* and it is openly discussed and valued. The trend in the professional coaching world is to hire young coaches who can communicate and relate to their players and who understand the value of a strong and positive team culture.

A recent example is the Los Angeles Rams football team who in 2021 were the NFL Super Bowl Champions. They were coached by Sean McVay, who at age 36, became the record-holder for the youngest head coach in NFL history to win a Super Bowl. Currently, there are five head NFL coaches who are in their thirties.

I am a big Minnesota Vikings fan and in 2022 they hired a new head coach. The coach they hired was Kevin O'Connell who, before he was hired by the Minnesota Vikings, was the offensive coordinator of the Super Bowl

Champions Los Angeles Rams. I remember hearing Kevin O'Connell's first press conference, and here was his quote:

"When we got to talking football, we got to talking about a shared core vision of what we want our football team to look like. It's our job to take the team we put together and put it on the field and best execute game plans and put them in positions to have success, but there's got to be collaboration. That's the number one thing that I think that we talked about—that we're so excited about, is through the process of getting to know each other. We've known from day one that we're going to be able to collaborate, communicate with one another and build a culture here that the players will feel. They'll feel a connectedness between Adofo-Mensah's (Vikings General Manager) staff and our coaching staff, and that will only lead to the players feeling as connected as they've ever been to a coaching staff before."

When you break down and analyze what Coach O'Connell had to say, you will see that he knew the importance of not only building a team culture but an organizational culture that focused on a shared vision, collaboration, and communication. Today, in the coaching world, building a strong, positive organizational culture is seen as extremely important. For today's professional coaches, their most important job is building culture, and it is no longer seen as something that just happens but something a coach must intentionally build.

Fortunately for me, when I was hired as a dean, I was aware of how the leadership world was changing and the importance of building caring, collaborative work environments. As a result, I spent much of my time as a dean reading to learn more about how to lead and how to build a strong, positive organizational culture. What I learned in the process was that most organizational leaders, like coaches, know that culture plays a significant role in helping any organization succeed, but most leaders fail to take the time to truly develop an understanding of organizational '*culture*', and the steps needed to build it.

Climate and Culture

If you were to review the literature in the field of organizational culture, you would find that the terms *'culture'* and *'climate'* are defined differently but are interdependent. However, you will find in conversations among organizational leaders and in practice, these terms are often used interchangeably, which can hinder an understanding of organizational culture.

For example, as a member of the North Dakota Every Student Succeed Act (ESSA) Implementation Committee, I was asked to be on the state's ESSA School Climate subcommittee. In North Dakota K-12 schools, *'school climate'* is one of the criteria used to assess a school's effectiveness. The ESSA School Climate subcommittee is responsible for defining school climate and providing insight to the implementation committee into how to measure it in our state's K-12 schools.

The process we went through to arrive at a workable definition and then finding and developing a valid assessment instrument to assess school climate was extremely time-consuming and difficult. The subcommittee first tried to create a working definition of school climate that could be understood by all stakeholders, but little did we know how difficult this task would be.

During this process, it became clear that committee members believed the terms organizational culture and climate to be not only interchangeable but meaning the same thing. As I mentioned previously, these terms are interdependent, but there is a difference in how each is defined and their influence on how organizations function.

Literature on organizational behavior supports the concept that culture is a subset of climate with climate most often defined as the total characteristics or overall atmosphere of the organization. Organizational climate includes everything from the interpersonal relationships of the people in the organization to the buildings, equipment, and furniture that can influence the perceptions employees have about the organization.

Culture, on the other hand, is the shared values, norms or standards that determine how people behave in the organization. Unlike climate, culture is much more difficult to observe and identify, because it is based on the actions and beliefs of the people in the organization that are often not exhibited directly through their behavior.

To help understand the difference between culture and climate, I have found it helpful to think of the human body, with climate as the body and culture as the body's veins and arteries. Culture – the veins and arteries of the body – keep the body going by bringing nutrients to its vital organs. If the blood in a body flows sluggishly or if something hinders its flow, the body or climate weakens and becomes fragile. If this happens over time, the body will become prone to illness and might even die.

Like the human body, organizations with a poor or weak blood flow or *'culture'* are more than likely not functioning as effectively as they could be if they had a strong blood flow or culture. People in organizations with a weak culture may do their jobs but are rarely motivated or inspired to perform at a high level or give their best effort. The organization may appear healthy from the outside, but internally is unhealthy, prone to making bad organizational decisions and likely to have a lack of trust between management and employees, increased employee turnover and decreased employee motivation and engagement.

During my tenure in higher education, I have taught master's level courses on school leadership and school administration and a doctoral course on organizational behavior. In teaching these courses, I immersed myself in the literature on how organizations function and how organizational culture is built. During this process and through my own experiences, I learned that building a strong positive organizational culture begins by having a leader who believes in the value of building a strong positive organizational culture.

If a leader wants to build a strong and positive organizational culture, the leader must first believe it is a worthy and important endeavor and not a waste of time. The organizational leader must not only believe in its importance but must become the culture-building cheerleader and spokesperson.

Any leader who wants to build a strong, positive organizational culture must also understand that a leader can only do so much because culture is built primarily by the social environment created by both spoken words and unspoken behaviors of those in the organization. Leaders who understand this know that, although they might be the spark needed to create a strong positive culture, it is the people in the organization who are the fuel needed to ignite the organization's culture and bring it to life.

As a result, selecting people to join an organization should be of utmost importance because its people will make or break a leader's ability to develop a strong, positive organizational culture. The members of any organization will be the force that brings culture to life, not the leader because a culture that is lived by those in the organization always trumps the leader's influence.

Defining Organizational Culture

In one of my graduate courses, one of my textbooks is *Organizational Behavior in Education* written by Owen and Valesky. In this textbook, *culture* is defined as, "*the values, belief systems, norms, and ways of thinking that are characteristic to the people in an organization.*" A key phrase in this definition is the phrase '*ways of thinking.*' When I read these words, they jumped off the page for me because for the first time I began to see culture as a living thing and not only as how an organization sees itself but as what it believes about itself.

As I mentioned at the beginning of this chapter, Edgar Schein is one of the most well-known authors in the study of organizational culture. He has been studying organization since the 1980s, and his work has provided significant insights into the world of organizational culture with his definition of organizational culture as one of the most comprehensive I have read. He defines culture as:

"The accumulated shared learning of that group as it solves its problems of external and internal integration, which has worked well enough to be considered valid and, therefore, to be taught to new members as the correct way to perceive, think, feel, and behave in relation to those problems. This accumulated learning is a pattern or system of beliefs, values, and behavioral norms that come to be taken for granted as basic assumptions and eventually out of awareness."

Organizations that can solve problems, create change, innovate, and create have what I call a *dynamic* organizational culture, an organizational culture where people embrace change and innovation.

But even organizations with strong and positive organizational cultures include people who resist or fight change. As human beings, we like stability; the status quo seems less stressful because it helps make us feel safe.

However, in today's world, change is inevitable. Without change, an organization will be less likely to improve and innovate and, therefore, be more likely to fail. If any organization wants to create a culture where change is a way of life, it must transform its organizational culture from *static* to *dynamic,* where change is embraced and accepted.

Building a Dynamic Organizational Culture in Education

In 2023, the National Center of Educational Statistics (NCES) reported that since 2010, the national college enrollment rates for high school graduates declined from 68 percent to 62 percent, and from 2019 to 2021, declined more than 4 percentage points, from 66.2 percent to 61.8 percent. The data appears to indicate that high school graduates are considering other options after graduating from high school rather than attending college.

In 2013, the New York Times published an article by Clayton M. Christensen and Michael B. Horn titled *Innovation Imperative: Change Everything*. In this article, the authors predicted that due to decreased high school graduation rates, the increase in for-profit universities and the expansion of online education, *"...a host of struggling colleges and universities — the bottom 25 percent of every tier, we predict — will disappear or merge in the next 10 to 15 years."* They continue, *"... those that truly innovate — fundamentally transforming the model, instead of just incorporating the technology into established methods of operation — will have the final say."*

If the data from NCES and Christenson and Horn's thoughts are accurate, higher education institutions need not only to build a strong positive organizational culture, but they must build a *dynamic* organizational culture, that is, an organizational culture open to change and innovation if they want to survive.

In the current competitive higher education market, academic institutions are continually required to focus their energy on reaching their enrollment goals. With this daily focus, it is vitally important that higher education institutions develop a *dynamic* organizational culture, so administrators and faculty are actively engaged in innovation and finding creative ways to solve enrollment, recruitment, and retention problems as they arise.

As Peters and Waterman stated in their 1982 book, *In Search of Excellence,* successful organizations have a consistent common thread:

"The power of values and culture in these corporations rather than procedures and control systems provides the glue that holds them together, stimulates commitment to a common mission, and galvanizes the creativity and energy of their participants."

Although Peters' and Waterman's research is almost 40 years old, their findings are still true today. Every leader must remember that their organization's culture is the wind behind its sails, and it is truly what makes organizational members move boldly forward with the energy and creativity needed to help the organization succeed.

When thinking about how to define a *dynamic* organizational culture, I failed to find any authors who used this adjective when defining organizational culture. However, for me, the term '*dynamic*' clearly identified the organizational culture I wanted to build in our school and was significantly more important than just building a positive organizational culture. A *dynamic* organizational culture, I believe, is what is needed not only in today's higher education but in almost any organization today that is trying to compete in a highly competitive market. As a result, the definition I created for defining a *dynamic* organizational culture was:

"An organizational culture in which people are encouraged to innovate, a culture where change is expected and where members of the organization all share the belief that it is important to take risks, to embrace challenges and to dream big."

In my definition, the values of innovation, taking risks, embracing change, and dreaming big, I believed would help our faculty and staff better define what is acceptable behavior in our school and what is a good idea, what is a bad idea, what is possible and what is not possible. In a *dynamic* organizational culture, people are eager to be innovative; they understand that change is part of the culture. As Dean, a *dynamic* organizational culture was what I wanted to build in our school, and I was determined to make it happen.

Literature in the field of organizational behavior supports the notion that culture is the *'social control system'* used by leaders to help the organization meet its goals. An organization's social control system can be used to engage people emotionally, provide them with direction, give them a sense of purpose, and empower them to improve their performance.

The social system created by the members of an organization provides the norms and values of the organization, significantly increasing member commitment to the organization. The social system provides organizational members with an understanding of *"how things are done around here."*

In K-12 schools and higher education institutions, the organization's culture or social system is often seen as the *'hidden curriculum'*. The written curriculum, that is, the lessons, courses and learning activities that students are engaged in, is not solely what produces or increases student performance. Student performance is also influenced by the hidden curriculum, that is, the beliefs of teachers, staff and administrators about students and their day-to-day interaction with students. The hidden curriculum is what truly increases student performance and student learning. It is what differentiates effective K-12 schools or higher education institutions from those less effective.

In a final analysis, a *dynamic* culture is built through the invisible social contract that is signed by all members of an organization and becomes visible through the social interactions of the people in the organization and the organization's willingness to embrace change and innovate.

As Schafer states: *"A culture will be strong or weak depending on the interactions between people in the organization. In a strong culture, there are many overlapping and cohesive interactions, so that knowledge about the organization's distinctive character and what it takes to thrive in it is widely spread."*

A *dynamic* organizational culture is fueled by the values and beliefs shared among the people in the organization - the bricks that form the culture's foundation. In organizations with a strong organizational culture, key words, stories, and the values shared by its members will become part of the organizations' DNA. So, I knew if I wanted to build a *dynamic* organizational culture where our faculty and staff believed in *'change,' 'innovation,'* and *'taking risks,'* these words would have to become our shared values and lived by everyone in our school.

University of Mary's Organizational Culture

At the University of Mary, our mission statement is *"To serve the religious, academic and cultural needs of the people in this region and beyond."*

Our mission arises from the commitment of the Benedictine Sisters of Annunciation Monastery, who founded the University in 1959 and continue to sponsor it today. At the University of Mary, those who visit our campus can clearly hear, feel, and see our mission and values as a Christian, Catholic, and Benedictine institution. We have artifacts displayed throughout our campus that clearly identify to visitors, our students, faculty, and staff who we are.

Every candidate who interviews for a position at the University of Mary is required to write a Mission Reflection Paper. Institutional administrators are required to read each candidate's Mission Reflection Paper for the sole purpose of determining if the candidate is a *'good fit'* for our institution. However, being a good fit does not mean they must be Catholic or even Christian. A good fit means the candidate can wholeheartedly support our mission and they will feel at home in our community and a place where they can thrive and grow.

Hiring people who are a good fit is extremely important, demonstrated by the fact that each candidate is interviewed by our President, regardless of their position. Our President reads each candidate's vita and Mission Reflection Paper and then conducts his own personal interview with each candidate.

Upon completion of the President's interview, our President contacts the hiring manager to provide feedback about his support or lack of support for hiring the candidate, as well as his personal perceptions of the candidate. The feedback we have received from the President is extremely helpful and allows us to boldly move forward, offer the candidate a contract and let them know we want them to become part of our University of Mary community.

The University of Mary takes seriously its responsibility to articulate our mission and values to anyone who applies for a position. We want all applicants to truly know and understand our organizational culture and determine for themselves if the University of Mary would be a good fit for them. Institutional fit is a vital part of our hiring process, taking center stage in all discussions with candidates.

The values we share as a community are based on our Benedictine heritage and the following six Benedictine Values:

Community - Striving together for the common good and growing in relationship with God, one another, and self. "Let all things be common to all." (Rule of Benedict 33)

Hospitality - Receiving others as Christ with warmth and attentiveness. "Let all be received as Christ." (Rule of Benedict 53)

Moderation - Honoring all of God's creation and living simply with balance and gratitude. "Regard all things as sacred and do everything with moderation." (Rule of Benedict 31)

Respect for Persons - Recognizing the image of God in each person and honoring each one in their giftedness and limitations." Honor everyone and never do to another what you do not want done to yourself." (Rule of Benedict 4)

Service - Meeting the needs of others in the example of Jesus the servant leader. "The members should serve one another." (Rule of Benedict 35)

Prayer - Attending to the mystery and sacredness of life, abiding in the divine presence, listening, and responding to God. "Listen intently to holy readings. Give yourself frequently to prayer." (Rule of Benedict 4)

As our President, Monsignor James Shea, has stated, *"Although communal life inspired by the Rule of St. Benedict stores a vast treasury of Benedictine values, Community, Hospitality, Moderation, Respect for Persons, Service and Prayer are of particular importance for our life at the University of Mary."*

In addition to the Benedictine Values, there is also a focus on *'Servant Leadership.'* Students at the University of Mary can participate in service-learning experiences essential to becoming a servant leader. Students have the freedom to discover their gifts and develop critical leadership characteristics, so that they may find personal fulfillment while serving others. All students are encouraged to see themselves as whole and unique individuals responsible to God and to become *'leaders in the service of Truth.'*

An example of this is the University of Mary Day of Service, which is a student-driven initiative to promote community and foster servant leadership among students, staff, faculty, administration, and alumni. It is the largest one-day charitable service event in North Dakota. The Day of Service was started in the summer of 2014 by members of the University of Mary student government who wanted to develop a tradition encompassing the university's Benedictine values. The students wanted to create a 'community learning day' where students, faculty, and staff volunteer to participate in service-learning projects on campus and off campus within the Bismarck-Mandan community.

In the inaugural year, the Day of Service had over 700 students, faculty, staff, and administrators volunteering in the Bismarck-Mandan community at over 55 different sites. Since then, the day has grown to include over 1,300 volunteers. In addition to the Bismarck-Mandan community, satellite University of Mary campuses, including Fargo, ND, Billings, MT, Tempe, AZ, and Rome, Italy, participate in the day to give back to their communities.

Each year, the Day of Service begins on campus with a prayer service and convocation and keynote address. The University of Mary volunteers board buses and spend the day volunteering for various service-learning projects in the community. The mission of the University of Mary Day of Service is to light a desire among students, faculty, staff, administration, and alumni to dedicate their lives to serving others.

Value of An Organization's Artifacts

Schein viewed an organization's culture as not only the values and assumptions held by the organization but also its artifacts, the overt physical and social elements of an organization's culture. Schein believed an organization's culture is evident through the display of its tangible and intangible artifacts. Tangible artifacts are the physical objects that can be found throughout the organization, such as awards, mementos, logos, and marketing materials. And intangible artifacts are the stories told by organizational members and the words they use in their everyday social interactions and interactions with those outside of the organization.

In my 30-plus years at the University of Mary, I have accumulated various tangible artifacts. The tangible artifacts I have collected are on display in my office and represent noteworthy events I have been involved in at the University of Mary. For example, I have a miniature handbell that represents the university's 50th anniversary; a plaque recognizing my years of service to the university; a candle from the opening of the Lumen Vitae University Center; a coffee mug with the NCAA Division II logo marking when we joined NCAA Division II, and an empty bottle of champagne from the celebration of our school's first doctoral program, an Ed.D. in Educational Leadership.

In the center of my display is a picture of Sister Thomas Welder, who served as our President from 1978 to 2009. Sister Thomas was an iconic figure, a true servant leader, a person of remarkable character and a role model for all of us. Sister Thomas passed away in 2020, but she will never be forgotten by anyone who knew her, whether you were a University of Mary student, faculty member, or staff member.

Sister Thomas was a walking and talking intangible artifact who was eager to share stories about our university. Sister Thomas could recall events and discussions with others with ease and each story she told would leave you with a better understanding of who we were and our values as a higher education institution and learning community.

For an organizational leader who wants to build a *dynamic* organizational culture, it is important they understand the power of an organization's artifacts and how they can significantly influence its members attitudes and beliefs. I have never seen or worked in a more mission-focused and value-driven institution like the University of Mary. We know who we are, what we believe, why we exist, and are not shy about telling others.

You can see our tangible artifacts throughout campus in every classroom and all meeting areas. And include a crucifixion icon that is displayed in most classrooms and meeting places, the University of Mary for Life logo, the iconic capital M with a cross, and our colors of blue and orange. The intangible artifacts are evident in the interactions of our community members and the words they use with each other and those who visit our campus.

The University of Mary is mission-focused and driven by its core Catholic, Christian, and Benedictine values, which has influenced me immensely and had a major influence on my work as a dean.

Chapter 1 – Lessons Learned

In the world of sports, coaches have always known the value of team *'chemistry'* or a team's culture is important in building a winning team.

Most leaders know the value of a strong organizational culture, but very few know how to define *'culture'* or understand how to build it.

An organization's *'culture'* is what will determine if the organization succeeds or fails.

Organizational culture in simple terms is defined as *"The values shared by people to help them understand how we behave and how we do things around here."*

A *dynamic* organization culture encourages *innovation* and sees *change* as a way of life and is defined as, *"An organizational culture in which people are encouraged to innovate, a culture where change is expected and where members of the organization all share the belief that it is important to take risks, to embrace challenges and to dream big."*

When trying to build a *dynamic* organizational culture, leaders must remember that the *'social environment'* created by its members will have the biggest impact.

Organizational leaders must not forget the power of *'artifacts'* when developing their organization culture because an organization's artifacts are tangible and intangible symbols of its culture and can significantly influence its members attitudes and beliefs.

Chapter 2

Step 2 – Develop a Leader-Leader Mindset

"The function of leadership is to produce more leaders, not more followers."

– Ralph Nader

There are currently more than 15,000 books on leadership in print, including New York Times bestsellers. A brief list of the top-selling books includes:

- *On Becoming a Leader* by Warren Bennis
- *Good to Great: Why Some Companies Make the Leap ... and Others Don't* by Jim Collins
- *The Leadership Challenge: How to Make Extraordinary Things Happen in Organizations* by James Kouzes and Barry Posner
- *Start with Why: How Great Leaders Inspire Everyone to Take Action* by Simon Sinek
- *Dare to Lead* by Brene' Brown
- *The Effective Executive: The Definitive Guide to Getting the Right Things Done* by Peter Drucker
- *The Infinite Game* by Simon Sinek
- *The 21 Irrefutable Laws of Leadership: Follow Them and People Will Follow You* by John C. Maxwell
- *Extreme Ownership: How U.S. Navy SEALs Lead and Win* by Jocko Willink and Leif Babin

- *The Five Dysfunctions of a Team: A Leadership Fable* by Patrick Lencioni
- *The Advantage* by Patrick Lencioni
- *Humble Leadership: The Power of Relationships, Openness, and Trust* by Edgar H. Schein and Peter A. Schein
- *Tribal Leadership Leveraging Natural Groups to Build a Thriving Organization* by Dave Logan, John King, Halee Fischer-Wright
- *Courageous Leadership* by Bill Hybels
- *Leading with the Heart: Coach K's Successful Strategies for Basketball, Business and Life* by Mike Krzyzewski
- *Man's Search for Meaning* by Viktor Frankel
- *The Trust Edge: How Top Leaders Gain Faster Results, Deeper Relationships, and a Stronger Bottom Line* by David Horsager
- *Small Acts of Leadership: 12 Intentional Behaviors That Lead to Big Impact* by G. Shawn Hunter

People in leadership roles in any organization are sometimes desperate to find that *'magic bullet'* that will help them lead their organization more effectively. However, as Michael Shinagel, Dean of the Division of Continuing Education and University Extension at Harvard University, states, *"Despite the popularity of the topic, leadership remains a paradox. People who seek to understand it by reading a primer on the topic will inevitably be frustrated and disappointed. Leadership, after all, is an art, not a science."*

I agree with Shinagel that leadership is an art, not a science, and, as a result, every organizational leader needs to figure out for themselves how they plan to effectively lead their organization. There is no specific leadership style or philosophy that will work for all leaders. Each leader must develop their own unique leadership philosophy that best fits who they are as a leader and guide their leadership actions and decisions.

To become successful, leaders need to keep learning and find the leadership style and philosophy they believe in and will guide them as leaders. If a leader wants to inspire others, they must become authentic leaders. That is, they must lead based on the leadership philosophy they believe in and the leadership principles that will guide them as leaders and bring out the best in others.

I have known only a handful of leaders who are guided by a strong foundational leadership style or philosophy of leadership. In fact, if you were to ask, "*Why do you lead the way you do?*" Most leaders would not be able to answer this question because they are leading without any thought as to the core principles that guide how they lead. Most leaders tend to lead as they were led, with very few ever taking the time to analyze their own leadership style, beliefs, or philosophy.

In my doctoral course, Administration and Organizational Behavior, one of the first assignments for students is to write a '*Theory of Practice*' paper. In this assignment, students are to reflect on how they plan to lead, deal with conflict, make decisions, and build a positive organizational culture. This paper also requires students to describe their leadership style and philosophy in detail.

What has been surprising to me is that most students say they have never thought about how they plan to lead. In fact, my students would often tell me this is the first time they have been asked this question, even though they all have master's degrees and usually in an educational leadership position.

Very few students have a clear understanding of leadership and a core understanding of the beliefs and principles that will guide them. They all want to become effective leaders, yet most have not even taken the first step, which is to develop a good understanding of how they plan to lead by developing a leadership style or philosophy that is aligned with their belief system and their past leadership experiences.

Learn to Lead by Leading

My first teaching and coaching position out of college was as a physical education teacher, athletic director and head boys' basketball coach at Seoul Foreign School, a private Christian school in Seoul, South Korea. I was recruited to teach and coach at Seoul Foreign School in 1977 during my last semester of college. At this time, there was no email, a phone call from Korea back to the states cost a couple of dollars a minute, and mail took two weeks to deliver.

So, I began my teaching and coaching career in a foreign country with little ability to visit with any of my mentors. I was on my own, except for the support of a group of first-year teachers. We grew together as teachers and slowly found our teaching legs, but not without our struggles and failures.

As a first-year teacher and coach, my teaching and coaching styles were to teach as I had been taught, and coach as I had been coached. However, I quickly discovered that I was, indeed, a rookie coach and had much to learn about both teaching and coaching. In my first year as a head boys' basketball coach at Seoul Foreign School, I somehow managed to help my team get five wins. I still feel sorry for the players on that team, having me as a rookie coach.

After my first year of teaching and coaching under my belt, I took the time to analyze my own teaching and coaching philosophies. As a teacher, I decided to think less about lesson planning and, instead, spent more time asking myself, *"Are my students learning anything?"* As a result, I slowly began to enjoy teaching again because I had more of a focus on my students and less of a focus on me.

As a coach, I conducted a self-analysis by reviewing the previous year's practice plans. I also spent time in self-reflection and asked myself the following questions:

- *What do I believe about leading others?*
- *What are my coaching beliefs and principles?*
- *How can I inspire my players to help them reach even higher levels of performance?*
- *What is my offensive and defensive coaching philosophy?*

My self-analysis revealed that nothing I was doing was authentically me; I was merely coaching from my college coach's playbook. So, for the first time, I started asking myself what I believed about myself as a coach, what my personal coaching philosophy was, and what coaching principles I honestly believed in. For me, this was my first transformational leadership moment, and it significantly changed my thoughts about leadership.

In my second year as a teacher and coach at Seoul Foreign School, I grew as a teacher, a coach and, most importantly, as a leader. I fell in love with coaching all over again. I was beginning to understand who I was as a leader and what I believed about teaching, coaching and leadership. More importantly, however, I was enjoying teaching coaching again. Why? Because I was more authentically me, in my approach to teaching and coaching and, as a result, developed more confidence in who I was not only as a teacher and coach, but as a leader.

In my second year of coaching, I enjoyed having one of my best seasons as a head basketball coach. We returned a couple talented players from the previous year, but we also had other talented players join our team. These players were the sons of missionary families who, the previous year, were in the United States due to their parents being on furlough.

With my coaching transformation and the addition of these talented players, my second season as a head basketball coach was a tremendous success. We went undefeated and won not only the Korean American Interscholastic Athletic Conference (KAIAC) Champions but won the Far East Basketball Tournament, a boys' basketball tournament for the top private and Department of Defense schools in East Asia.

Seoul Foreign School had never been invited to this tournament. To win it was truly unthinkable because only the top eight boys' basketball teams in East Asia were invited to this tournament. My transformation as a coach that year helped me become a better coach. Even though my players had the talent to win it all without me, I believe being the best version of me as a coach and leader allowed my players to reach their full potential as individual players and as a team.

Without going through a failed first year as a head boys' basketball coach, my transformation as a leader and coach would never have occurred. Instead, I learned from my first-year coaching failures and became a more effective coach, which allowed my players to achieve something which they had only dreamed about. Without my coaching transformation, you would not see in the Far East Boys Basketball record book *'Seoul Foreign Crusaders - 1980 Champions'*.

A side story about this team is that a few years ago, I got a call from one of the players from that team. He was one of the boys who was on furlough my first year but joined our basketball team in my second year as the head boys' basketball coach. He was from a family from Kentucky that loved basketball and whose father was an avid Kentucky Wildcat fan.

He was traveling from Idaho and passing through Bismarck on his way to visit his family in Kentucky. He asked if I had time to have dinner with him. Of course, I jumped at the opportunity because, although I had stayed connected with a couple of members of that team, I had not talked to this particular player since leaving Seoul Foreign School in 1980.

My wife and I met him for dinner, and we reminisced about our experiences at Seoul Foreign School and our championship year. At one point in the conversation, he paused and said,

"Coach, I do not know if you know this, but my dad passed away last fall, and I regret not telling him before he passed how thankful I was for all he did for me. So, that is why I contacted you and asked if we could have dinner together. I wanted to thank you for all you did for me." To which I responded, *"You are welcome."*

This story is an illustration of the power and influence of every leader and how, even at the initial stages of my leadership journey, the influence I had as a leader and coach. At the time, I did not understand the influence I had on my players, but this experience motivated me to focus more of my time and energy on becoming a stronger leader and inspiring others to lead. I knew this was especially important in the leadership development of our faculty members, who as teachers, had the ability to significantly influence the development of the students in our school.

Servant Leadership

When I was hired as Dean of the Liffrig Family School of Education and Behavioral Sciences, based on my experiences as a first-time head basketball coach, I decided to intentionally take the time to learn how to become an effective educational leader. I had held other administrative positions at the University of Mary, but none of those positions required the administrative, management and leadership responsibilities I now had as a dean.

Fortunately, as a professor and a graduate instructor, I have studied different leadership styles and reviewed and read textbooks on leadership. In addition, I had a good working understanding of Servant Leadership because of its emphasis at the University of Mary on inspiring our students to become servant leaders.

As I began to reflect on my role as dean, I knew I had to take another transformational leadership step. As a leader I became not only focused on being a *Servant Leader,* but a leader who could help others learn to lead and inspire others to help our school create a *dynamic* organizational culture. I knew it would be important for me to develop a leadership style that would allow others within the organization to lead because as an organization grows, a leader becomes less and less involved in the daily operations and, therefore, needs to rely on the people in the trenches to make the day-to-day decisions.

The faculty are the lifeblood of every effective higher education institution. The day-to-day work of teaching, student advising, and curriculum development is done by faculty. I knew that it would be impossible for me to develop a good understanding of each discipline in our school at the level needed to make good decisions. I knew I would need a leadership style that would give the faculty the authority to not only make decisions but to take on the leadership roles needed to create innovative academic programs and develop a *dynamic* organizational culture.

I wanted our faculty to become academic leaders who would take personal responsibility for program development and student enrollment and who embraced change and innovation. I wanted our faculty to become leaders of their programs, own their programs, and transform how we do the work of our school.

In his book, *Turn the ship around: How to create leadership at every level,* Captain David Marquet stated:

"The leader-leader structure is fundamentally different from the leader-follower structure. At its core is the belief that we can all be leaders and, in fact, it's best when we all are leaders. Leadership is not some mystical quality that some possess, and others do not. As humans, we all have what it takes, and we all need to use our leadership...People who are treated as followers have the expectations of followers and

act like followers. As followers, they have limited decision-making authority and little incentive to give the utmost of their intellect, energy, and passion."

These words are at the core of how I wanted to lead. I wanted to be a leader who would help our faculty grow as leaders and as professionals and a leader who would give faculty the freedom to use their imagination and creative skills to build the best academic programs in the region. I knew if I were to become a successful dean, I would need to embrace a *'leader-leader'* mindset and leadership style to bring our school's *dynamic* culture to life.

If you review the leadership research from the 1970s and 1980s, you will find the research usually has a *'contingency theoretical'* foundation; that is, research that focused on the traits, characteristics, and behaviors needed to become a successful leader.

When I was in graduate school pursuing a Ph.D., in one of my courses, I was required to take a leadership inventory that helped define the leadership traits and behaviors aligned with my leadership style or philosophy. Upon completion of the leadership inventory, you were defined as being a laissez-faire leader, a democratic leader, or an autocratic leader.

During that time, leaders were primarily defined by their leadership traits and characteristics and were pigeonholed into one of the three leadership styles. I have learned, however, that no leader can be defined as solely a laissez-faire leader, a democratic leader, or an autocratic leader. Why? Because good leaders use different leadership styles based on the situation, the characteristics of those they lead and the urgency of the task at hand. Effective leaders do not rely on one specific leadership style to deal with every situation that comes their way or, when making decisions or when working with others.

In recent decades, authors have begun to focus less on the traits or characteristics of leaders and more on the types of leadership philosophies, including situational, adaptive, transactional, visionary, servant, and transformational leadership philosophies.

Transformational Leadership

As I researched these various leadership philosophies, the leadership philosophy that resonated with me the most was the *'transformational leadership'* philosophy.

James Burns introduced the concept of transformational leadership and defined it as a process where *"leaders and their followers raise one another to higher levels of morality and motivation"*.

The transformational leadership philosophy is in direct opposition to the transactional leadership philosophy that I was used to, which focused on getting people to perform by granting or withholding rewards and benefits. The literature on transformational leadership supports the idea that leaders should spend their time building trust with the people in the organization, inspiring people to higher levels of performance, supporting innovation and increasing followers' motivation to improve. This leadership philosophy was aligned with, as a person, my own value system, and what I personally looked for in leaders who have led me.

Four major elements define transformational leaders: idealized influence, inspirational motivation, intellectual stimulation, and individual consideration.

- Transformational leaders' *'idealized influence'* comes from the leader's strong convictions and ethical actions. Leaders with idealized influence are positive role models whose followers respect and admire them because the leader is authentic and trustworthy.

- Transformational leaders exhibit strong *'inspirational motivation'* skills and the ability to inspire and motivate others because of their enthusiasm and optimism. These leaders are often charismatic, confident, can inspire confidence in others and clearly articulate a vision for the organization.

- Transformational leaders exhibit strong *'intellectual stimulation'* skills and are eager to involve followers in the decision-making process and encourage followers to be creative and innovative. They also have high expectations of their followers and want every follower to succeed.

- Transformational leaders demonstrate the ability to have *'individualized consideration,'* which means they have concern for everyone and work with followers to develop their leadership skills. Transformational leaders understand that each member of the organization has unique skills, strengths and weaknesses and are eager to help each follower reach their full potential and become valuable members of the organization.

In reviewing these elements, I knew I possessed many of these transformational leadership attributes and had a good vision for our school, worked hard, and had effective communication skills. These leadership attributes defined who I was as a leader and were attributes I believed in and defined me as a leader.

I wanted our faculty to be intellectually stimulated to innovate and create change in our academic programs. I wanted to treat each faculty member as a unique individual with unique gifts and talents. I thought I had the ability to inspire others, had some charisma and, along with a servant leader's heart, could make a difference in the lives of our faculty, staff, and students.

Leader-Leader Philosophy

As a result of studying both servant and transformational leadership philosophies, I developed my own leadership philosophy. I call my leadership philosophy a *'leader-leader'* philosophy because I wanted to view every faculty member in our school as a leader, no matter what position they held. I know I am the person at the top of our school's organizational chart, but I wanted our faculty to see themselves as leaders no matter where they were on the organizational chart so we could build a *dynamic* organizational culture that is adaptive and innovative.

I knew that building a *dynamic* organizational culture would not happen without me developing a leader-leader mindset and leadership philosophy. Without this type of leadership philosophy, I knew there was little chance for us to become the school I had dreamed of, one where faculty dreamed big, embraced challenges, and took the risks needed to move our school forward. I knew I needed to be surrounded by leaders, not just followers, and that my success as a leader hinged on my ability to recruit faculty who could lead with me.

At the time of my hire as Dean, President Monsignor James Shea rolled out the university's strategic plan called '*Vision 2030*', which included major school initiatives that I was expected to lead. So, I knew the next step for me, as a new dean, was to build a strong leadership team to bravely meet the challenge of achieving the Vision 2030 goals developed by our President Monsignor Shea and the Board of Trustees.

As a coach, I knew every good team was made up of talented players, and the best thing I could do as dean would be to focus my energies on finding key people who could help us build our school. I knew I needed to find passionate, committed, and mission-focused faculty who wanted the authority and the autonomy needed to build strong academic programs and who would thrive in a *dynamic* organizational culture.

I knew I needed to find faculty who would view their position as a vocation and not just a job. I needed to find team members who would embrace change, take risks, and work hard to help our school succeed. As the leader of our school, I also knew I needed to push authority down to those in our school who oversaw our various academic programs. I knew this would require hiring competent collaborative faculty who did not fear failure and who would boldly work to build strong academic programs.

Chapter 2 – Lessons Learned

Numerous books have been written on leadership because all leaders are looking for the *'magic bullet'* that will help them lead effectively. Unfortunately, there is no magic bullet. You need to build your own leadership philosophy that is based on your own belief system and the leadership principles you value.

Every effective leader has their own beliefs about leadership, but very few leaders have ever taken the time to develop their own *'Theory of Practice'* as to how they plan to lead others.

A leader's *'leadership philosophy'* will have a direct impact on the performance of people in any organization and their desire to innovate and change.

For any organization to develop a *dynamic* organizational culture that provides team members with the *'authority'* and *'autonomy'* to be creative, and innovative and the ability to create their own future.

Chapter 3
Step 3 – Build Your Team

"If you want to be great and successful, choose people who are great and successful and walk side by side with them."

– Ralph Waldo Emerson

As I planned to build our school team, I was keenly aware that our faculty came from different disciplines, including education, criminal justice, social work, and psychology. Except for the education faculty, the faculty members in our school rarely had the opportunity to work together and did not know each other and had no reason to trust each other.

As a result, I knew we would need to work at building trusting relationships and defining the roles of each faculty member. As the past Chair of the Department of Education, I was familiar with those programs and faculty; however, I was not as well acquainted with the faculty in criminal justice, social work, and psychology. So, I spent the first year as a dean trying to learn as much as possible about all the academic programs and building a relationship with the criminal justice, psychology, and social work faculty.

I also tried to develop a good understanding of each program's culture, how faculty solved problems and how they interacted with each other in finding solutions. It seemed like a simple task, but it proved to be more difficult than I expected. These faculty were not sure who I was as a person or how I planned to lead, and I knew their legitimate concern was whether they could trust me.

As Dean, I realized that only a limited number of our school faculty had worked together before, and, as a result, they saw themselves as nothing more than a '*group*' and not as a *'team.'* I knew building a dedicated team would take time and would only occur after the faculty had developed strong professional relationships with me and each other. I tried to consistently remind myself that, *"People don't trust people they don't know!"*

Prior to becoming a dean, I had spent much of my time with the education faculty but little time with the faculty in the other academic program areas that I was now entrusted to lead. In the Department of Education, I understood the processes used to *'get things done,'* but the same processes did not always seem to work with the other program faculty.

These faculty had their own culture and had been led by a chair whose leadership style was much different from my leadership style. I could tell they were watching my every word and action, trying to figure out how I led, and asking themselves, *"Can I trust him?"*

In my previous roles as Physical Education Program Director, Student Teaching Program Director, and Chair of the Department of Education, I worked with education faculty in curriculum development, faculty evaluation processes, writing accreditation reports, and dealing with program and student issues. Together we built strong education programs and developed a positive organizational culture. We knew each other's strengths and weaknesses and worked together effectively. At times, this familiarity made building our new team difficult because other school faculty often felt like outsiders, not part of our school team.

In meetings with our school's faculty members, I would often catch myself saying *'our programs'* when referring to education programs but not doing the same for the other academic programs. I tried my best to get those words out of my vocabulary, but the education faculty and I had been a team, and it was difficult for me not to look at them differently. At times, I became frustrated with myself for not connecting better with the other faculty members in our school, but as much as I tried to connect with them, at times, it seemed forced or fake.

So, I decided to give myself a break and just do my best, believing that with time, the faculty in the other academic programs would eventually see me as the leader of all our academic programs. I worked hard to get to know all the faculty members in our school, but I tried my best to remain authentic as a leader and just be me.

When I began to conduct a critical analysis of the faculty and staff in our school, it became clear to me that we did not have faculty with the breadth and depth needed to get the job done in meeting our Vision 2030 goals. That is not to say we did not have strong faculty members in the school. We just did not have enough of them with the necessary team mindset and leadership skills needed for us to build the *dynamic* organizational culture we needed to succeed.

What we needed most were more faculty members who wanted to own their academic programs and who would take the initiative to change and develop creative and innovative ideas on their own. We needed more faculty members who would help us move from a static organizational culture to a *dynamic* organizational culture and a team of leaders who had the skill and drive to inspire our faculty to implement the initiatives needed to meet our Vision 2030 goals.

In the department model, decisions were made at the presidential level, and the chair along with the department or program faculty, were expected to implement those decisions. In this model, faculty were given little autonomy and decision-making responsibilities. They were expected to teach well, but with the tacit implication to leave the rest to upper administration.

In the department model, the chair was not a true administrator but what I would describe as a *'facilitator.'* Chairs were not asked to be innovators or change-makers, so there was little reason for a chair to do anything that would affect the status quo.

In fact, when I was hired as dean, I remember during the interview with our President Monsignor Shea, at the end of the interview, he asked me if I had any questions. I responded with, *"Yes, I do. If you hire me as a dean, will I be given the authority to be a dean?"* My reason for asking was that I wanted to be given the responsibility and authority to make my own hiring and firing decisions, to develop our own initiatives and to be held accountable for doing my job.

After I asked him this question, he responded with, *"Of course, I want you to dream big, and I want you to do what you feel necessary to build a great school."* I followed up with, *"I'm in, let's go!"*

With the reorganization of departments into schools, the landscape had changed, and the expectations of a dean were to become the lead administrator for each school. As a result, moving from a chair position to a dean position, I had moved from being a facilitator to a true academic leader. I felt pressure, but I embraced the change and was excited to take on the challenges we would encounter.

Recruit and Hire People Who are a Great Fit

With the hire of a new president, our university became more innovative, and a culture of change was building because our president had a vision for the University of Mary that was going to require a commitment from everyone, especially from our academic leaders. It was clear that more academic and enrollment responsibilities were going to be given to deans, and more would be expected of us than was ever expected from a person in a chair position.

I knew I needed to improve my leadership skills because I was about to take on challenges that were outside of my areas of expertise and past leadership experiences. I realized I needed to become a much stronger leader and would need to inspire our faculty to even higher levels of performance, as well as recruit and hire faculty who were open to change and motivated to lead the new initiatives that we were expected to implement. I needed to hire more faculty members who embraced change and not fearful of change, and who could help our school move from a static culture to a *dynamic* culture, one in which people were given the authority and autonomy to build, create, and own their academic programs.

Without this *'culture shift,'* I knew we were likely to fail, and, for me, failing has never been an option and is simply not acceptable.

As I was learning how to be a dean and how to lead more effectively, I got involved with *'Growing Leaders,'* a nonprofit organization that partners with schools, colleges, athletic departments, and other organizations to develop today's emerging generation of leaders.

My connection with Growing Leaders started because of the development of the Emerging Leaders Academy program in our school. This program was designed to help students in their personal and professional development. It was not an academic program, but a program designed to help our students develop the personal and professional skills and attitudes needed to become successful professionals and leaders with moral courage.

To learn more about how to help the students in our Emerging Leaders Academy grow as leaders, I enrolled in one of one of the Growing Leaders' summer leadership conferences. The conference included presentations by leaders from various organizations who spoke about how to become effective leaders and about their own leadership journeys. At this conference, I met Dr. Tim Elmore, CEO, and founder of Growing Leaders and we talked about how our Emerging Leaders Academy and how we could build our academy to better equip our students with the skills and attitudes needed to become successful people and professionals.

The following year, I invited Dr. Elmore to conduct a workshop for students in our Emerging Leaders Academy. At the leadership workshop, Dr. Elmore talked to our students about what he called the *'Habitudes'* needed to help them become effective leaders and to help them learn how to navigate life's challenges and opportunities. He spoke to our students about how they are each on their own personal leadership journey and the importance of viewing leadership as art rather than a science because there is no perfect script a person can follow to become an effective leader.

My involvement with Growing Leaders and Dr. Tim Elmore spurred me on to think more deeply about the leadership skills I needed to become an effective leader. More importantly, however, it helped me to begin to think more deeply about the need for hiring faculty who could lead alongside me because I knew I could not be successful without a talented team of faculty. I knew I needed highly qualified faculty with the appropriate degrees and experiences in their discipline, but I often asked myself, *"What other qualities did they need to have to help us create the dynamic organizational culture needed to help our school grow and flourish?"*

As I reflected on my high school and college coaching career, I knew coaching had taught me that winning was more fun than losing and, if you wanted to win, you needed talented players.

At the end of one championship season at the University of Mary, I asked one of my assistant coaches to review the previous year's game tapes and see if he could find the reasons our offense was so effective.

The previous year, we had won the conference title and participated in the district tournament, and we had no problem scoring no matter who we were playing. At the end of the week, my assistant coach showed up in my office and said, *"I found out why we were such a good offensive team."*

"Well, what did you find?" I asked. His answer was "Rory Entzi."

Rory was our best player and was the second-all-time scorer in men's basketball history at the University of Mary.

I had been thinking my assistant coach would uncover strategic offensive secrets we could use to improve the offense of future teams. What I found was that our success was the result of talented players and had little to do with coaching. I am not downplaying the importance of coaching, but the lesson learned here is that talented players trump good coaching.

Every year since I have reminded myself that success is the result of having talented players, so if an organization wants to be successful, it must find the best players for its team. As Dean, I knew if we had talented and committed faculty, anything would be possible, and success follows when you have talented players and teammates who believe in and trust each other.

When building our faculty team, a quote from Mike Krzyzewski from his book, *Leading with the Heart,* came to mind, "*Leaders have to search for the heart of a team because the person who has it can bring out the best in everybody else - including the leader.*"

As I looked back on my successful basketball teams, I realized that every one of those teams had a player who was the heart of the team, a player whose presence made the team better, a player who had the courage to dream big and who did not fear failure.

When I had teams with a player who others saw as the heart of the team, coaching was so much fun. Why? Because the stress of winning was not solely on my shoulders but was shared by our coaches and players. These types of players led by example, and other players took on their positive competitive mindset.

As I reflect on past teams, one specific player comes to mind as the best example of a player who was viewed by his teammates as the heart of the team. The player was Cory

Wilhelm, a member of our first championship team. Cory was truly our heart, not our best player, but the heart of our team. He was fearless, trusted by his teammates, and he loved competition. He also played with so much joy.

After one practice, I remember asking him why he never appeared nervous before games and why he was always so confident. His reply was: *"Coach, first of all, I love playing basketball, but second I never really think about what happens if we lose, instead, I try to think about what happens if we win."* And you know, that is exactly how he played; he worked hard, did not make excuses, and never feared losing. I am so grateful for having coached him and I am a better leader and person because of having the opportunity to coach him.

Recruit Great Teammates

During the 2020 Summer Olympics, I spent time watching the USA women's Olympic volleyball team matches. I had watched a documentary on the team prior to the Olympics. The documentary included interviews with Head Coach Karch Kiraly and key players on the team. The documentary provided insight into the team culture and documented the journey of these women and their quest for an Olympic gold medal. Coach Kiraly talked about the sacrifices these women make, the double lives they lived, being on professional volleyball teams for half the year and the other half playing for and training with Team USA.

Listed below are players' quotes from the documentary that provide a glimpse into the culture created by the USA Women's Olympic Volleyball team.

"You must be willing to give everything you have and ... in turn, that just narrows the field to those people who just soak up life and it makes a very great environment."

"Stay open to feedback, open to trying new things and not having crazy expectations but going with the flow."

"All 23 are like all TEAM first. It is incredible."

"It's not like we need everyone to be the same level of competitive or the same level of ... whatever, but we need everyone to recognize what their strengths are and how can I contribute those into the group effort."

"As a team we have really set ourselves up for success. We are trying to make history. We are one of the best teams in the world. Frikking, let's do it, that's exciting!"

Coach Kiraly talked about the *team's first* philosophy and said,

"We don't have a player on our team nor are we aspiring to have one that just is the whole team. Our best chance for success is really to 'out-team' everyone else."

When asked how they planned to win the Olympic gold, the players all used the same phrase: *"Out-team everyone else."*

And they did, winning the first gold medal ever by a USA women's Olympic volleyball team.

I wanted to build a team like that, a team of talented faculty members who were scholars, teachers, leaders, and change-makers who were passionate about the work they do. I knew if we could find the right faculty, our Vision 2030 goals would become a reality.

Unfortunately, I soon learned that defining the characteristics of the faculty I was looking for was much easier than hiring them.

I conducted a critical analysis of my full-time faculty and asked myself: *"Do we have the faculty currently on staff who could help build the dynamic culture needed to reach our Vision 2030 goals?"*. The answer emerged quickly when I asked faculty to take more ownership of their academic programs, the faculty in their programs and student enrollment. Most faculty members embraced their new role, but others did not. It was clear to me that I would need to lead this change and select faculty who wanted to lead and who wanted ownership of their academic programs.

The shift in organizational culture was easy for certain faculty and difficult for others. Most embraced their new roles with excitement and others did not. Our focus on change and innovation and building a *dynamic* organizational culture, although outwardly supported by the faculty, was difficult because it required our faculty to develop a different mindset than what currently existed in our static organizational culture.

During this time, faculty retired so we hired new faculty, but not the faculty I thought we needed to get the job done. I also knew we did not have any faculty member who could be described as the '*heart*' of our team. If we were going to help our school achieve its Vision 2030 goals, I had to recruit differently.

So, as I moved into my third year as dean, I began to mentally lay out a three-step faculty recruitment plan.

Step '*one*' was to determine what new initiatives and programs were going to be implemented in the next few years and the academic requirements needed by the faculty hired to fill new positions.

Step '*two*' was to clearly define the type of person needed to fill our open faculty positions, that is, faculty who had the mindset needed to thrive in a *dynamic* organizational culture.

Step '*three*' was to think more creatively about how to find the faculty we needed and not rely solely on the current recruitment process.

As we worked through these three steps, I began to work closely with our Human Resources Office so we could accurately describe in our position postings the type of person we were looking for. I also worked with my Academic Vice President to ensure we could offer the salary needed to attract the faculty we were looking for.

During the next year, we had two open faculty positions that included administrative and leadership responsibilities. I knew filling these two positions with the right people was going to be one of the most critical decisions I was going to make as a dean. Like my time as a basketball coach, I knew I needed to find players and, in this case, faculty members who had strong expertise as teachers and leaders. I knew that to be a credible leader our faculty needed to be led by people who were experts in the field, someone they admire and aspire to become.

I created a list of all the people I had been associated with during my tenure as Chair of the Department of Education and in my current role as dean who might be great candidates. My list included people I had worked with in K-12 schools, faculty from other institutions I had worked with, and professional organizations. I also added to my list anyone I had met at national conferences or served on state or national committees. I knew I needed to find two great teammates who were eager to lead faculty in the development of our new academic programs and who had the drive and passion needed for these positions.

One of the open positions was the Chair of the Department of Education, an especially critical position because this department had the highest enrollment and the largest number of faculty. The person filling this position needed to be a passionate educator with strong leadership skills who could inspire our education faculty to even higher levels of performance.

I also hoped to find a faculty member who was a strong administrator and who could be the *'heart'* of our team. In reviewing the candidates who had applied for this position, one candidate kept rising to the top. Dr. Brenda Tufte, a teacher at Bismarck High School in Bismarck, North Dakota, had a Ph.D. in Teaching and Learning and had been the cooperating teacher for a number of our English Education preservice teachers.

She had also taught courses for us as an adjunct faculty member and had done considerable adjunct faculty work for other higher education institutions. In 2012, she was selected as the North Dakota Teacher of the Year. Dr. Tufte was one of the top candidates on my personal recruitment list, so she was one of the first candidates interviewed by our search committee.

After we conducted candidate interviews, it became clear that Dr. Tufte was the best candidate for the position. My only worry was how we were going to get her to accept a faculty position at the University of Mary. She loved teaching and was making a salary that I assumed we would have a tough time matching because of her Ph.D. and years of service in the Bismarck Public School District.

Despite my concerns, I scheduled a dinner with her and Dr. Becky Salveson, the Chair of our Graduate and Distance Education Programs. We met at a local restaurant, and we talked for a couple of hours about the state of education, her interest in this position, her salary range and, if she was selected, her goals for our education program. Her responses to each question were not scripted but from the heart and aligned with what we were looking for in building our *dynamic* organizational culture. It was clear she would be a terrific addition to our team.

At the end of the dinner, I asked her if she was interested in the position. She paused slightly, then said, "*Yes, I'll take the position. When can I interview with the President?*" I nearly fell off my chair because, at that moment, I realized we had found the *'heart'* of our team. Dr. Tufte was confident, fearless, innovative, and someone who was eager to take on the challenges of our Chair position.

The next step in the hiring process was to schedule a meeting for Dr. Tufte with our President, Monsignor Shea. The President's interview was scheduled for 30 minutes, but an hour passed, and Dr. Tufte was still in the interview. I became a little nervous and thought to myself, "*Why is the interview taking so long?"* Finally, Dr. Tufte emerged with the President from his office. Both were laughing and smiling, which was a relief. I ushered Dr. Tufte to my office and I told her I would need the President's final approval before I could offer her a contract, but I hoped that I would get his approval in a day or two.

The very next day, I received a phone call from Monsignor Shea. He said, *"I have never had a better interview with a candidate than I did yesterday with Dr. Tufte. She will be a terrific addition to your school."* He then said, *"How did we get her? Wouldn't a person like her have other job opportunities?"* I responded with, *"I'm not sure. I think it is a GOD thing!"*

Dr. Tufte was the heart we were looking for, my Cory Wilhelm. Cory made me a better coach, Dr. Tufte was going to make me a better dean.

The next open position was the Chair of our Graduate and Distance Education because Dr. Becky Salveson, a very competent administrator and teacher, was retiring. The responsibilities of this position were enormous because of our school's Vision 2030 goal to develop a Doctorate in Education.

Again, I knew I needed to find a talented leader who had the grit and leadership skills needed to make our Doctorate in Education a reality. Dr. Tufte had raised the bar, but finding someone with similar qualities was now my focus.

One day, as I was reviewing my candidate list and thinking about other potential candidates, I came to the name Dr. Carmelita Lamb. I paused and thought to myself, *"Dr. Lamb is the answer to my prayers."*

Dr. Lamb was the Chair of the Teacher Education Program at Turtle Mountain Community College in Belcourt, North Dakota. I had collaborated with her as a member of the North Dakota Association of Colleges for Teacher Education (NDACTE) and was extremely impressed with her commitment to teacher preparation at Turtle Mountain Community College [TMCC] and its Native American students. She was a strong advocate for Native American education and appeared to be a competent educator and administrator.

In North Dakota, every tribal college had a teacher education program, but apart from Turtle Mountain Community College (TMCC) had very few graduates. TMCC had teacher preparation programs in Science and Elementary Education, and I had heard students from TMCC give presentations at the annual NDACTE Conference and was extremely impressed with their content knowledge and teaching skills.

Dr. Lamb's students not only graduated but were competent pre-service teachers. I saw how proud she was of them and the respect they had for her. She not only the skills and knowledge we needed but also the grit and perseverance needed to help our school implement the graduate initiatives we had on the horizon.

As I began to check references and talk to people about Dr. Lamb, I became even more impressed because of the things I heard about her. I learned that Dr. Lamb was not only a great teacher and administrator but also a great person. I heard stories about her life and tragedies she had encountered in her own family.

Dr. Lamb had been through tough times, yet appeared to have found the inner strength to persevere and seemed to focus on her blessings and not the problems she encountered in her life. For me, this spoke volumes about her character and who she was as a person. I was impressed by what I learned about Dr. Lamb, and I made the decision to recruit her as a candidate for the Chair of our Graduate and Distance Education faculty position.

The following semester, we held the annual NDACTE Conference on our campus and at the lunch break, the attendees were walking on our campus's beautiful Sage Path, which overlooks the Missouri River, one of the best scenic views in North Dakota.

I purposely walked alongside Dr. Lamb. As we were walking, I mentioned that we were starting an Ed.D. program at the University of Mary and had just opened a Chair of Graduate and Distance Education position and that the person selected for this position would be guiding this effort. I then asked her if she would consider applying for the position and leading our Ed.D. program development. After an endless pause, she looked at me and said, "*I would.*"

Inside, I was bursting with excitement. I could not believe that this was happening again. Well, that spring semester, Dr. Lamb agreed to become an administrator in our school and university community and, along with Dr. Tufte, has been a major force in helping us develop the *dynamic* organizational culture I had envisioned.

Dr. Lamb was the second piece of the puzzle, and along with Dr. Tufte, helped jump-start our school on a new trajectory. She has been a key role model for our junior faculty because she is a great team player and teammate, a gifted administrator and leader, and a wonderful person. Her work is not about her but about her students, especially our Native American students.

I remember, before she signed her contract, she indicated she would be willing to come to the University of Mary under one condition: that she would be allowed to continue writing grants for Native American students, so they can earn a University of Mary degree. Well, my answer of course, was, "*Sure, feel free to write as many grants as you want.*"

Little did I know how passionate Dr. Lamb was about supporting the Native American community and helping students earn college degrees. During her tenure, Dr. Lamb has written $10 million in grants and has helped more than one hundred Native American students earn their doctoral, master's and bachelor's degrees from the University of Mary.

I am so proud and grateful that Dr. Lamb chose to become part of the University of Mary community.

These two faculty members were the major building blocks needed for our school to move ahead and build the dynamic culture we have today. Without these faculty on our administrative team, I have no idea where we would be today.

As I mentioned in Chapter 1, when building a strong positive organizational culture, a leader can only do so much; the culture really comes from the social environment of those in the organization.

Well, Dr. Tufte and Dr. Lamb changed our school's social environment from one of *'maybe we can do this'* to *'of course we can do this.'* They were the faculty members we needed to show those who joined our school *'how we do things around here.'* They embraced the goals outlined in Vision 2030 and never showed a fear of failure. They are true servant leaders, and I thank God every day for having the opportunity to work with these passionate and selfless leaders.

Create a Recruiting Process and Philosophy

With Dr. Tufte and Dr. Lamb on board, the next few years became a whirlwind of new initiatives and the addition of new faculty. With the success of hiring these two great colleagues, I began to ponder how we could make this happen again.

I quickly learned, as a leader, that it was all about finding the right people, people who are a good fit and who would be attracted to the University of Mary because of our values and culture. I knew that the more faculty we had, like Dr. Tufte and Dr. Lamb, the more likely we were to attract other highly qualified and talented faculty.

Using the lessons learned in recruiting Dr. Tufte and Dr. Lamb, I collaborated with the administrators in our school to refine our school's recruitment and interview processes. As I began to think about the recruitment process, I was reminded of a documentary I watched on the building of Apple's Macintosh computer. I had shown this documentary to students in a school administration class because it focused on the importance of hiring great people.

I watched the documentary again. It was titled *Teamwork - The Steve Jobs 1985 Macintosh Computer Team*. The video starts with an interview with Steve Jobs, where he talks about finding the right people to build the Macintosh. Jobs stated:

"We wanted people who were insanely great at what they did, but were not necessarily seasoned professionals, but who had ... passion [and] the latest understanding of what technology was and what we could do with that technology and wanted to bring that to lots of people. So, the next thing that happens when you get a core group of ... ten great people, is it becomes self-policing as to who they let in that group. So, I consider the most important job of someone like myself is recruiting."

In the documentary, various members of the Macintosh building team discuss the interview process they used to select members for the Macintosh team. Macintosh team members talked about having candidates meet all members of the team once or twice to make sure they found someone they wanted on the team and that when the team felt they had found a suitable candidate, they would show them the Macintosh prototype.

In one clip, Andy Hertzfeld, a software engineer, said, *"If they were just kind of bored and said this is a nice computer, we didn't want them. We wanted their eyes to light up and get really excited; then we knew they were one of us."*

This is the type of recruitment culture I wanted. I wanted our faculty to take ownership of the recruiting and hiring process and take pride in finding and hiring faculty who were one of them and who would help us grow and improve. I wanted them to find faculty who fit on our team and who they would be proud to call a teammate.

As we developed our school's hiring process, we intentionally chose to keep the faculty interview committee members, primarily from our school. We wanted our faculty to find people who would be a good fit and, just like the Macintosh team, find faculty members to join our team who *'were one of us.'*

We take immense pride in the recruitment and hiring process and full responsibility for the faculty we select. As a result, our faculty members have become the biggest supporters and strong mentors of our new faculty. I have learned that when faculty own the hiring process, they become invested in the faculty we hire and do what they can to help that person succeed.

To assist our faculty in the interview process, I developed a set of interview questions to help determine the candidate's institutional and school fit. Throughout my career in higher education, I have been part of numerous candidate interviews, but found these interviews often failed to tell me much about the candidate. I would leave these interview sessions lacking enough information to really know if the candidate was the right candidate for the position.

I knew, for our school, interviews were extremely important and the best way for us to determine if a candidate was a good fit; therefore, I believed we needed to develop a more formal interview process that included asking the right interview questions to determine if the candidate was someone who would be a good teammate.

I his book, *The ideal team player: How to recognize and cultivate the three essential virtues: A leadership fable*, Patrick Lencioni states, *"First, we go figure out how to recognize a real team player, the kind of person who can easily build trust, engage in healthy conflict, make real commitments, hold people accountable, and focus on the team's results. Then, we stop hiring people who can't."*

Based on the belief that hiring the right people was one of my most important responsibilities, I developed a set of interview questions that I believed would help us determine if a candidate is a good fit and a good team player. Although we already had a set of interview questions that were mission-focused, I decided to include team-focused interview questions.

Below are examples of the types of questions our school uses when interviewing candidates to determine if they are team players.

- *In our school, we value working together as a team. How would you make us a stronger team?*

- *If you had a conflict with another faculty member, how would you resolve that conflict?*

- *Tell us about a co-worker from a previous position that made you a better faculty member and describe how he/she helped you in your professional development.*

- *Tell us how you have helped a colleague in a previous position become a stronger and more effective professional and teammate.*

- *Describe the leadership style of the leader in your current or last position. Did his/her leadership style help you become a better professional? Why or why not?*

- *If a student in your class was not performing well, what would you do to help that student succeed?*

Our interview process gives our faculty ownership of who joins our team. It is also a subtle reinforcement to the faculty of who we are and what we want in a faculty member. I consistently let our faculty know that they were all selected to be part of our team because of their unique skills and abilities. I also let them know that if each faculty member embraces their role, we will succeed together. If we make a mistake in selecting a candidate who does not possess the skills and characteristics, we thought they had, we own the mistake and work to help the faculty member succeed.

As Simon Sinek, author of *Leaders Eat Last: Why Some Teams Pull Together, and Others Don't,* explains, *"It is like when a player has a slump, we do not trade them, we coach them. It is the same with our employees. The best leaders come to the aid of their people, whose performance is down. Not come down harder on them."*

I wanted our faculty members to believe that when they collaborate with other faculty members in our school, to remember they are working with a teammate, and it is their job to help them improve. Whether they remain as faculty members is up to each individual faculty member because they will be given every opportunity to succeed.

Our hiring process is not foolproof. Not every faculty member we have hired has been a perfect fit, but our emphasis on selecting the right people has worked for us and has helped us hire faculty members who are not only competent and passionate about what they do, but faculty members who are team players.

As a result of hiring the right people, we have developed new academic programs in our school, and our student enrollment has continued to grow each year. In our school, we believe in hiring great faculty who are self-motivated and then removing the barriers that would hinder their ability to do their job.

As Simon Sinek was quoted as saying in his book, *Why: How Great Leaders Inspire Everyone to Take Action:*

"Great companies don't hire skilled people and motivate them; they hire already motivated people and inspire them. People are either motivated or they are not. Unless you give motivated people something to believe in, something bigger than their job to work toward, they will motivate themselves to find a new job and you'll be stuck with whoever's left."

As a result of our efforts, we currently have twenty-nine full-time faculty, all of whom have been hired during my tenure as Dean. Of the twenty-nine faculty members in our school, ten are men, and 19 are women, with an average age of around 45.

We have faculty with different religious beliefs and various ethnic backgrounds. We have faculty who had previous experiences in public education and Catholic private education, a faculty member who spends her summers barrel racing, a faculty member who acts in plays and musicals, faculty members who love to travel and write and others who enjoy the outdoors. We have an amazing group of diverse people with extraordinary gifts and talents who were all selected to play a role in our school.

As I have mentioned, when I was first hired as a dean, I sometimes felt out of my league, but I knew with a talented team of faculty to work with, we would succeed. Why? Because if we had faculty members who had the desire to be part of something bigger than themselves, who wanted to make a difference in the world and who wanted to become part of a successful team, anything was possible.

Create a Leadership Team

I am an avid reader of leadership books, and, as dean, I tried to get every leadership book I could get my hands on. One of the books I read was *The Advantage* by Patrick Lencioni. In his book, Lencioni focuses on the power of organizational health and begins with a chapter titled *"The Case for Organizational Health."* In this chapter, Lencioni has this quote, *"The single greatest advantage any company can achieve is organizational health. Yet it is ignored by most leaders even though it is simple, free, and available to anyone who wants it."*

Lencioni believes that any company or organization can achieve organizational health, yet most leaders ignore its importance and fail to take the time and steps needed to create a healthy organization. I knew I did not want to be one of those leaders. Instead, I wanted to create a school with a strong, positive, and healthy organizational culture.

Lencioni suggests that the first step for any leader in helping their organization become healthy is the creation of a leadership team to help lead the organization. Lencioni describes a leadership team as *"a small group of people who are collectively responsible for achieving a common objective for their organization."*

As I thought about the importance of creating a strong leadership team for our school, I knew it would change my role, and most importantly I would no longer have to lead alone. I already had Dr. Tufte and Dr. Lamb, who I trusted and believed in, but I knew we needed to build an even larger leadership team if we were to continue to grow and improve our school. I knew our leadership team needed to include all undergraduate and graduate department and program administrators.

My prior experiences as an administrator and coach have shown me that it is important to dream and to dream big. However, before a dream can become a reality, a leader must believe it can happen. What I have witnessed, however, is that for a dream to come to life, leaders should not just focus on the dream, but on the team that will make the dream come true. I believe that if you build the right team, the dream will always follow.

I have also noticed that good leaders surround themselves with competent people they trust and who are willing to tell them the truth. In the best organizations, leaders surround themselves with other great leaders who can assist them in dreaming big and sharing the pressures and responsibilities of leading their organization.

As a leader, I frequently must deal with difficult problems, and my first instinct on how to manage each problem has not always been accurate or well thought out and, as a result, often did not lead to the best solution. During my time as Dean, if not for input from a trusted teammate and colleague, I would have made fewer good decisions and more poor decisions. So, I have purposefully tried to surround myself with people smarter than me who were committed to our school and university and who were not afraid to tell me what I needed to hear.

I knew I needed key leaders and administrators in our school who had the courage to speak their minds and who could share information with me and each other for the betterment of the school. I needed a team made up of people who supported and trusted me and who had the courage to participate in difficult discussions for the purpose of making our school function more effectively.

I knew it was important to build a leadership team that could deal with sensitive organizational information. In past positions at the University of Mary and at various other institutions, leaders would usually only share sensitive information with certain people. There are legitimate reasons for not sharing personal or confidential information, but often, important institutional information was not shared either. I have been in meetings where I have heard upper administrators talk about issues and I have said to myself, *"Why did I not know this?"* Without accurate or complete information, how can I or anyone in a similar position make good decisions?

During these types of meetings, when I would hear information for the first time that was relevant to my position, I often felt as if I were not part of the team or a member of the *'inner circle'* or *'circle of trust.'* If I were part of the team, this information would have been shared with me.

Likewise, I have been in meetings where administrators were making decisions with bad information because they were talking to the wrong people or only trusted the opinions of certain people in key positions within the organization. Neither of these scenarios is healthy and was something I wanted to avoid. I did not want secrets in our school. Secrets can cause organizational dysfunction by sowing distrust between people who are on the same team.

I wanted a leadership team with whom I could share information and who were willing to share information with me so we could make good, prudent decisions. I wanted my leadership team to be people who spoke the truth, who were willing to tackle problems and who were not fearful of saying things that could be controversial or difficult to hear. I wanted our leadership team members to be people who were willing to openly express their own feelings and thoughts.

A concrete example I often use with my leadership team to illustrate the importance of team members being willing to share information and building trust is to think of this scenario. Pretend we are all riding in a car, and I am the driver. If one of the passengers hears an unusual noise from the car, don't you think it is important for them to say, *"What is that noise?"* Isn't it important for me, as the driver, to know something is making a noise so we do not risk having an accident?

Just like the driver of a car, leaders do not hear or know everything that is going on in the organization. Organizational leaders need people around them who are willing to let them know what is going on so that they are fully informed and can make the best decision possible for the organization.

However, in organizations with a low level of trust, where those in the car do not see themselves as part of the team, the people in the organization tend to just ride along, not letting the driver or anyone else know they hear a noise. In these organizations, even if the driver does hear the noise and asks the passengers what they think it is, the passengers may not even offer an opinion. Why? Because they do feel part of a trusting team.

As Simon Sinek states, *"A team is not a group of people who work together. A team is a group of people who trust each other."* In our school, I wanted to build a leadership team made up of faculty who trusted each other and would have the courage to tell me when they hear a noise, and not only tell me, but give me an opinion of what they think the noise is.

I know it can be often difficult for people to determine what to share with others in an organization. However, in our school, I wanted to know what is going on, so I could make the best decisions possible. I wanted leadership team members who would keep me and the other team members in the loop because the more information we had, the better decisions we would make as a leadership team.

To emphasize this point, I continually remind our leadership team members to look under the hood. Organizations can be falling apart, their engines smoking, but the leader who does not look under the hood does not even know it. Instead, they trust only their own ears or listen to a limited number of people to gauge what is happening in the organization. If you never look under the hood, it is often too late to repair the engine when it breaks down. This is how organizations function often function. Information is not openly shared because leaders hoard information or only share it with a selected few.

The opposite, however, can also be true and that is, people who know what is going on do not share information because they do not feel part of the team. People in this situation just do their job, stay in their lane, and are rarely honest and open and tell others what is truly on their mind. If I had recorded the number of times, I have heard people in organizations say, "*I just keep my head down and do my job,*" or "*I only work here,*" it would have been in the hundreds.

In the book *Turn the Ship Around: How to Create Leadership at Every Level,* David Marquet tells the story of a submarine sailor who, after receiving an order from the captain that was impossible to do, still barked out the order to his comrades in the submarine. When learning it was an impossible order, the captain asked the sailor why he would try to follow such an order. The sailor replied, *"Because it is my job to follow orders."*

This scenario happens all too often in organizations where there is not a high level of trust. I wanted to build our leadership team with faculty who were empowered and challenged to be leaders and not just followers. As David Marquet states in his book, *"I believe that rejecting the impulse to take control and attract followers will be your greatest challenge and, in time, your most powerful and enduring success".*

I wanted to build a school where my leadership team members were faculty who did not just follow orders, but who not only had control of their own work, but who were passionate and empowered to do their best and to give their best. I wanted my leadership team to have the right information so together could make the best possible decisions. I wanted them to feel confident to speak up, to not be afraid to look under the hood, and to trust each other enough to be willing to share information so we could make the decisions needed to help our faculty do their jobs.

My Starting Five

As a basketball coach, at the beginning of each season, I had to pick a starting five. With minimal exceptions and barring injuries, my starting five remained the starting five for the remainder of the year. The starting five represented the players who gave us the best chance of winning the game and were seen as the team leaders. This is not to say the other team members are not important, but without a strong starting five the chances of success will be limited.

Our school's leadership team is my starting five. I knew our school's success was going to hinge primarily on their ability to lead and inspire the faculty they supervised. Although they all had their strengths and weaknesses, I believe these starting five were collectively going to make a difference and help us meet our Vision 2030 goals.

At the Liffrig Family School of Education and Behavioral Sciences, I consider my current leadership team members to be my starting five, and they are:

- Our center was Dr. Carmelita Lamb, but she made the decision to retire this past year, so we set out to find another center. However, the reason I labeled Dr. Lamb as our center is because she was our enforcer, the person who kept us all on task and doing our job. Dr. Lamb was respected by every member of our school because of her devotion to our university and our students. She was selfless and brought in millions of dollars in grant monies to support the education of our Native American students. Dr. Lamb was our go-to person when we had a problem or when we ran into a personnel issue because she bravely took on any issue or problem that came her way.

  Our new center is Dr. Matt Lonn, who joined our school as the Chair, Graduate Education this past year. Dr. Lonn earned his undergraduate degree in Social Studies Education and his Ed.D. from the University of Mary, and his past administrative experiences include Director of the North Dakota Center for Distance Education and assistant principal in the West Fargo Public School District. We hired Dr. Lonn because of his strong leadership skills and work ethic, but, primarily, because we knew he would be a great fit for our school. He has been a fearless leader who believes in himself and those he leads. In his first year, he has already made a difference by implementing new program procedures and has eagerly taken on every task he has been given.

- Our point guard is Dr. Brenda Tufte. Dr. Tufte is our worker bee, the one who gets things done. Dr. Tufte has boundless energy and always has a cheerful outlook and a smile on her face. Dr. Tufte is an exemplary teacher and a strong leader. She believes in herself and always seems to find the best in others. As

I mentioned, she is the heart of our team and such a good role model for our faculty. I have worked alongside many wonderful people throughout my career, but to this day I can honestly say that Dr. Tufte is the smartest and nicest person with whom I have ever worked. It is never about her, but always about our students and our faculty. We would not be where we are today without Dr. Tufte becoming part of our leadership team.

- Our shooting guard is Dr. Kim Marman. Dr. Marman is always on top of her game. She stays abreast of what is happening in the field of teacher preparation and is continually looking for ways to improve our education programs and the skills of our preservice teachers. Dr. Marman has strong interpersonal skills and a high level of emotional intelligence. She has developed a great rapport with the faculty in her department. The faculty members she supervises believe in her and trust her because they know she is a true servant leader who leads with a servant's heart.

- Our forwards are Heidi Nieuwsma and Dr. Christina Jurekovic. Heidi Nieuwsma has an M.S.W. degree in Social Work, and Dr. Jurekovic has a Ph.D. degree in Counselor and Counselor Education. As a result, they often see things from a human behavior perspective, which allows them to give our team a different point of view when we discuss problems or are developing strategic initiatives. Together, they keep our starting five on their toes and their perspective on any given issue often gives us a unique perspective to think about. They have made us a stronger leadership team and they help our team find positive solutions to the problems we encounter. They do not even know this, but I call them '*our bookends*' because they hold us all together.

Our starting five are not great just because of their individual strengths, but because of their strong belief in each other and their decision to trust each other. Their team chemistry brings out the best in each other and helps us work together for the common good of our school and to help us build our *dynamic* organizational culture.

Chapter 3 – Lessons Learned

Leaders who want to build a *dynamic* organizational culture cannot do it by themselves; they need a dedicated team behind them.

When building your team, leaders must remember that it is extremely important to select people who are a *'good fit'* for your organization's culture.

As a leader, the first step in building a team is to find a person who will be the *'heart'* of the team, the person who, by their example, sets the standards for what is acceptable teammate behavior.

As a leader, make sure you know what characteristics you are looking for in a prospective candidate, so you can determine if a candidate would be a *'great teammate.'*

When interviewing candidates to be on your team, make sure to ask the *'right questions'* to ensure the candidate will be a good fit and a good teammate.

Your team should help decide who becomes a member of their **TEAM**.

When building a *dynamic* culture, it is important to create a *'leadership team'* because you need people around you who will tell you the truth.

An organization's leadership team must have the courage to *'look under the hood'* so they can continually check to make sure the organization is functioning at the highest level possible.

Chapter 4
Step 4 – Develop your TEAM Leadership Principles

"The single biggest way to impact an organization is to focus on leadership development. There is almost no limit to the potential of an organization that recruits good people, raises them as leaders and continually develops them."

– John Maxwell

Experience has shown me people are often put in leadership positions with little leadership training or understanding of how to lead effectively. Most leaders lead as they were led. Very few develop a personal leadership philosophy or an understanding of the principles that will guide them. So, as John Maxwell's quote highlights, the single biggest way a leader can impact their organization is to focus on leadership development, which includes the development of leadership principles that will guide your leadership team. As a result, one of the first tasks I started to work on with my first leadership team was the development of a set of leadership principles we would use to guide us.

Although the team members of my first leadership team had different leadership experiences and styles that would benefit us as a team, I knew we needed a common set of leadership principles we all believed in if we were truly going to lead our school effectively. Our leadership team members had great expertise in their fields, but few had administrative or leadership experience. So, as we came together, I stressed the importance of developing a set of leadership principles we could all believe in, which could be used as our own evaluation tool to help us assess our leadership effectiveness. Our team's leadership principles, I believed, would provide us with a road map of how we planned to lead as a leadership team.

Define Your Team's Leadership Principles

When trying to determine the leadership principles that would guide our leadership team, I reflected on the leadership books or leadership articles I had read. As I reflected on the content of these books, however, I realized that most leadership books and articles primarily focused on the value of communication, creating a shared vision, listening, having the courage to lead, walking the talk, passion, self-awareness, motivation, self-improvement, collaboration, and delegation. Although these are all helpful traits, none of the books I read focused specifically on the importance of leaders developing a set of leadership principles to guide them.

As I mentioned in the previous chapter, I enrolled in one of one of the Growing Leaders' summer leadership conferences to learn more about leading. At this conference, Joel Manby, at the time the CEO of Herschend Family Entertainment, the largest family-owned theme park corporation in the United States, was one of the speakers. During his presentation, he spoke about his book '*Love Works: Seven Timeless Principles for Effective Leaders*' that focused on how leaders can bring love, the verb, into the leadership ethos and philosophy of any organization.

Manby spoke about his leadership journey at the Growing Leaders Conference, and I remember how refreshing it was to hear from a humble leader who thought more about his people than he did about himself. His presentation was not the typical one that emphasized how to lead but about his own personal leadership journey and the values and principles he learned during that journey.

I purchased the book at the conference and read it from cover to cover the first night I returned home. As I thought about this book, I kept saying to myself, "*Why am I trying to reinvent the wheel?*" The leadership principles outlined in this book were aligned with my own personal leadership philosophy and were the leadership principles I believed fit who we were as a leadership team.

At one of our leadership team meetings, I brought copies of Manby's books for my leadership team members. We scheduled a meeting to discuss in detail the book's leadership principles, namely, that leaders need to be patient, kind, trusting, unselfish, truthful, forgiving, and dedicated.

At one of our follow-up meetings, I listed on a sheet of paper the leadership principles I thought we learned from reading the book together. At this meeting, I asked: *"What do you think? Does this accurately describe our leadership principles?"* I anxiously waited for a response. After a short pause, Dr. Tufte said, *"These leadership principles seem to fit who we are as leaders"* and everyone else followed with a similar response.

We discussed each leadership principle listed, edited each to fit who we were as a school and then listed them in a language that spoke to us so they would be owned by each member of our team. Next, I put our leadership principles in a poster format and made a framed copy for each of our team leaders.

Although the individual members of our leadership team have changed throughout the years, each member of our leadership team has a copy of this poster on their office wall or desk. To this day, our leadership team continues to be guided by the leadership principles we initially developed, and they have served us well.

These leadership principles have been extremely important in helping us to lead as a **TEAM** of leaders. They have become the rudder of our ship, and every new member of our leadership team gets a framed copy to place on their office desk or wall. These leadership principles are also listed on our leadership team meeting agenda each month to remind us of what we believe in as leaders, so we can effectively lead our faculty and staff.

We also have these leadership principles listed on our leadership team meetings that we call our *'Coffee Break.'* Our coffee breaks are not meetings, but a time for us to get together to discuss the problems and issues team members are dealing with so we can help each other make the best decisions possible and find solutions to problems we encounter as a team. The coffee break agendas are fluid, and we all own the agenda, and each leadership team member can edit or revise the agenda as needed.

Our coffee breaks provide a venue for our leadership team members to discuss things with each other in an open and honest manner. As a result, our leadership team meetings have become primarily informational sessions to keep us informed as to what is happening at the university and our coffee breaks are now where our real *'leadership'* work is done. Our coffee breaks have had a significant impact on our ability to build our *dynamic* school culture because it has provided time for our leadership team to dig deep into personnel issues and find plausible solutions to school problems.

Below is a list of the leadership principles we developed to guide us:

- Do the right thing, even if it is hard to do.
- Take the time to praise real effort and achievement.
- Lead with patience and respect.
- Let faculty make the decision for which they are responsible.
- Lead selflessly – think less of what is best for you and more about what is best for our school, our faculty, and our students.
- Deal with conflict – get the truth on the table.

Do the right thing, even if it is hard to do so

This leadership principle came from a discussion on the importance of leaders doing the right thing, which in our school meant doing what is best for students, our faculty, and our institution.

In his book, Manby said, *"...we achieve profits by doing the right thing for customers and employees; profits are not an end in themselves. Profits are a product of doing the right thing – over and over again."*

This leadership principle is not doing what is best for us but doing what is in the best interest of our students, faculty, and staff because our leadership responsibility is to do what is best for those we serve. Doing the right thing is the difference between being a *'manager'* and being a *'leader.'* As Warren Bennis, author of "On Becoming a Leader," states, *"The manager does things right; the leader does the right thing."*

The only question for our leadership team was, *"How do we know what the right thing is to do?"* Together we developed a simple measuring stick to determine if something is the right thing to do. We simply ask ourselves: *"Is this what is in the best interest of our programs, our faculty, and our students? If so, then it is the right thing to do."* We embraced this idea and knew that if we continually did the right thing, we would succeed, and our school would be able to achieve its Vision 2030 goals.

Take the time to praise real effort and achievement

We knew it would be important to recognize the achievements of our faculty and students. It is only through the achievements of those we serve that we will be able to know if we, as leaders, were truly doing our jobs. We believed that celebrating the success of our school's academic programs, faculty members, and student achievements would result in even more success for our school. However, we did not want to celebrate everything because then our celebrations would become fake or meaningless. We wanted to celebrate real achievements, that is, those achievements that took real effort. In his book, Manby states,

"To be truly effective, praise must be legitimate and pointed. Will everyone have good reason to believe this praise is true? What exactly is praise for? In other words, I can walk around town with a megaphone, praising my employees at the top of my lungs, but if what I say isn't believable and specific, it won't have the effect I want."

We took this to mean we should celebrate those achievements that were significant markers of the success of our programs, our students, and our faculty.

A simple idea our leadership team uses at each of our monthly school meetings, is to intentionally take time to celebrate an academic program achievement or a faculty achievement. We decided to place on the school meeting agenda, the term '*kudos*' right after our opening prayer or reflection. This is a time for any faculty or staff member to announce a program or faculty achievement so we could celebrate together as a school team.

A meeting rarely goes by when one of our leadership team members or another faculty member does not provide a kudo to a member of our school team or an announcement of a recent school or program achievement. I am often surprised by what I hear because I learn about faculty and student success stories that would have otherwise gone unnoticed, if not for a team member letting us all know. The kudos agenda time is motivating, builds trust, and models the behavior of showing appreciation for the work of others.

Another example of taking the time to celebrate real achievements is the University of Mary's annual Student Awards Banquet, held each year at the end of the spring semester. It is a simple celebration, but it provides an opportunity for the entire university community and our faculty to celebrate the achievements of our undergraduate students. Our school's program directors have created academic awards that highlight the academic achievements of our undergraduate students in each of our academic program areas.

The awards banquet is not only a time to celebrate with our students but helps our faculty members reflect on the tremendous work they do and demonstrates the difference they are making in the lives of their students. This event is also a wonderful way to say goodbye to our students and thank them for giving us the opportunity to teach and mentor them during their time at the University of Mary.

As I mentioned earlier, I have a collection of artifacts in my office celebrating specific achievements. One is an empty champagne bottle. This bottle may seem out of place, but for me and our graduate faculty, it represents a tremendous achievement. It is a bottle of champagne we shared after receiving notice from the Higher Learning Commission that our doctorate in education, our Ed.D., was approved, a goal of ours since officially becoming a school.

This was an endeavor that took two years to achieve and a tremendous amount of work and sacrifice from Dr. Lamb, Dr. Tufte and our graduate education faculty. It might be just an empty bottle to most people, but for our graduate faculty and our leadership team, it represents the significant effort and the *dynamic* organizational culture we created to make this happen.

Every time I see that empty bottle, I feel immense joy, because it reminds me of what can happen when a team is committed to a goal and to working together to achieve something great.

Lead with patience and respect

Because we often had new junior faculty on staff, who had never been in higher education before, our team often discussed the need for patience. We also realized no one is perfect and that we all make mistakes. To build confidence in our faculty, we knew we needed to give them room and time to grow.

In Manby's book, he focuses on the value of patience in a leader in the chapter titled: *"Patient: Have Self-Control in*

Difficult Situations." In this chapter, Manby discusses a personal story of being reprimanded by a CEO and having to reprimand people when he was President and CEO of Herschend Family Entertainment. In these situations, he stresses the importance of the leader being patient and treating employees with respect and love because the goal of every company is not, as he says, "*...simply performance; it's to protect the dignity of the people on the team ... handling difficult situations with patient admonishment is a sure sign of leading with love.*"

After reading this chapter, I had a new perspective on my role as a leader. Our school had new initiatives to implement, and our faculty and our leadership team members were in uncharted waters. We knew we needed to be patient with our faculty, giving them the time needed to help us move these initiatives forward. These initiatives often took a tremendous amount of planning and collaboration. Expecting our faculty to implement these initiatives overnight and to see immediate results was unreasonable. Patience often gave us the time to alter or revise our plans and '*do the right thing.*'

Our institution had lofty expectations for student enrollment in our school and our team knew that if we expected to meet these lofty goals, patience would be needed. For a private institution like ours, students are the main source of revenue. Without revenue, we knew we would not be able to do the things we had envisioned. In my role as Dean, I knew the pressure for student enrollment was real, and how we dealt with this as a leadership team would invariably affect our faculty's reaction to these pressures.

Each month, my leadership team and I attend an enrollment task force meeting focusing on enrollment goals and initiatives. The first agenda item is always our current enrollment numbers and where we are in relation to our enrollment goals. Because of the meetings' pointed focus on enrollment, it is easy to get caught up in the numbers and lose patience and perspective when those numbers are down.

As leaders, however, we knew our faculty were committed to increasing enrollment and truly felt that a never-ending focus on enrollment numbers would only cause stress. So, we had to find a way to lead with patience and not get too focused on numbers only.

Dr. Tufte is the best example of how to lead with patience and respect. She continually stresses to our faculty the need to see the big picture and to remember when enrollment in one program is down, often the enrollment in another program is up. She continually reminds our faculty, *"Our school's student enrollment goals are not the responsibility of one program or one person. It is the responsibility of all of us and together, we will meet our enrollment goals."*

Dr. Tufte's calming voice has been a healthy reminder that, although enrollment is important, it is not the most important thing to focus on. Instead, she has taught us to keep focused on doing our jobs, working together and being there for our students. If we do, things will work out. She has been right; we have met our school's enrollment goals every year, mainly because our sole focus has not been on numbers but on working together and sharing the responsibility of enrollment with each other.

The second part of this leadership principle is to lead with respect. Our leadership team members understand that we are all uniquely different people. We might look at things differently, but if we respect each other even when we disagree, we can help each other grow and work together effectively as a team.

We also believe that mutual respect helps us build stronger professional relationships and helps create the social environment needed to build feelings of trust, safety, and well-being. *'Respect for Persons'* is one of the Benedictine values of the university and, as a result, this leadership principle is something we believe in and demonstrate each day at the University of Mary.

Let faculty make the decision for which they are responsible

Three quotes in Manby's book reinforced the value of this leadership principle for our school.

The first quote was "...*trust people until proven wrong.*"

The second was "...*the fewer decisions we feel we need to make, the stronger a leader we are and the stronger team we have built.*"

And the third was, "*I try to hire only the best – and then I let them do their jobs.*"

These quotes were truly how we felt as a leadership team and became the impetus for including this as one of the principles that should guide us as leaders, especially because of our leadership roles in higher education. In higher education, the term '*shared governance*' is a term used to describe the joint responsibility of faculty and administrators to work together to govern the university and, develop policies and make decisions that affect students, faculty, and the institution.

We wanted our faculty to have a voice in decisions that affect them and to build a collaborative process that included input from everyone affected by the decisions that are made. Our leadership team believed strongly in shared governance and in giving faculty authority to make the decisions needed to improve their programs. Thereby, giving them ownership of their academic programs would help us build the dynamic culture we were trying to develop.

We passionately believed that giving authority to those with the academic knowledge and expertise needed to make these decisions would demonstrate our trust in our faculty and increase their commitment to our school, our academic programs, and our students.

Leaders often fail to delegate or fail to allow others to make decisions because they feel the need to be in control or enjoy the power of making decisions. Not allowing others to make decisions can also come from fear of failure and a lack of trust in others.

When I first became Dean, I must confess that I was guilty of all of these. In the beginning, I needed to be in charge and, if I were honest with myself, even enjoyed the power in the position. I was worried about failure, and I did not have complete trust in my faculty.

However, as we grew as a school and selected competent faculty members to become part of our school, I eventually gave the authority and power to make academic program decisions to my leadership team members and faculty in program director roles. I have had faculty who have made poor program decisions, but by allowing them to fail and giving them the autonomy to do the job that they were hired to do, they have become stronger leaders and administrators.

I can honestly say that today, I am doing only 70 percent of what I was doing 10 years ago and making almost no academic programming decisions. Our faculty, and in particular our chairs and program directors, make these types of decisions because they are on the ground level doing the work. They are experts who understand their programs, faculty who I trust, believe in, and hired.

As a result, I spend my time focusing on developing new initiatives and partnerships and helping remove barriers so faculty can do their jobs. I am routinely now in meetings where I ask myself, *"Why am I here?"* because I realize *"They don't need me!"*

Early in my career, this feeling would have caused me to worry or think I was not doing my job. Today, however, it makes me smile because I know that our *dynamic* culture is working, and we will be a better school because of it.

Lead selflessly – Think less of what is best for you and more about what is best for our school, our faculty, and our students

Robert Greenleaf, the author of several books on servant leadership, defines servant leadership as *"... a philosophy and set of practices that enrich the lives of individuals, builds better organizations and ultimately creates a more just and caring world."*

At the University of Mary, the emphasis on servant leadership is the legacy of our beloved past President, the late Sister Thomas Welder. Loved by generations of students and faculty, she was a shining role model of selflessness and humility. Sister Thomas talked often about servant leadership and would challenge leaders when she spoke on servant leadership with these questions:

"Do those you serve grow as people because of my leadership?"

"Do they become healthier, wiser and more likely to want to serve?"

"Does your leadership serve to build community?"

The idea of being a servant leader, however, is easier said than done. I have learned that when dealing with an issue or tackling a problem, all leaders tend to view the issue or problem through their own lens. It is human nature to do so. But we knew as a leadership team, we each had to put our own selfish desires aside and do what is best for our school, our faculty, and our students.

Fortunately, our leadership team had no better teacher than Sister Thomas. If we planned to be effective leaders, we knew we could not be selfish or self-centered. We needed to become '*servant leaders*' and focus our energies on inspiring our faculty to serve our students through the development of strong academic programs.

Deal with conflict – Get the truth on the table

In organizations where conflict flares up weekly, even daily, a leader's time can often be engulfed with managing conflict. Conflict can destroy the organization's culture if it is not dealt with appropriately.

As a leadership team, we knew we needed to learn how to deal with conflict if we were going to become an effective leadership team. In his book, *Five Dysfunctions of a Team*, Patrick Lencioni stresses the importance of leaders being able to manage conflict. He stresses that effective teams must not only deal with conflict, but they must embrace it by learning how to not only give but also receive honest feedback.

I have attended meetings where I could feel the tension in the room, where the people in the meeting did not feel safe talking about the conflict. They often felt this way because of their position in the institution. Or because of who else was in the room, such as a person who had supervision responsibilities over them or someone with whom they needed to maintain a strong relationship with to do their job. In these cases, people rarely spoke the truth or gave their honest opinion.

This is why I tell my leadership team members they must develop strong relationships with each of their faculty members, so they are not afraid to let them know when conflict or problems arise. As I have mentioned, I consistently remind my leadership team members that *"People do not trust people they do not know."* So, you need to get to know each of the faculty members you supervise so you can deal with conflict effectively.

I also expect my leadership team members to fight for their faculty because faculty are often not able to fight for themselves. I have personally fought for faculty who made a mistake or who were in a tough situation due to an error in judgment. Why? Because I believed in them and did not want them to not take risks because of fear of making a mistake.

I have also fought for faculty just because I knew they could not fight for themselves due to their position. As their leader, if I did not fight for them, who would?

In university meetings, I have seen people do what I call *'prairie-dogging,'* a term I use to describe people in a meeting who have sunk quietly into their chairs and only popped their heads up when called upon.

Prairie-dogging is common in organizations where people do not feel safe or supported and who do not trust each other. In these meetings, you often sense that people want to speak up or know something that needs to be said. Unfortunately, most people rarely speak up because they fear being labeled as troublemakers or believe their thoughts or suggestions do not matter.

At the University of Mary, the Rule of Saint Benedict identifies *'murmuring'* as "*a malignant wound to common life.*" As a result, I think, at times, community members fear speaking up because their actions may be seen as not being Benedictine. However, if you go deeper into the Rule of Benedict, he also encourages humble, constructive, trustful raising of concerns. Yet, it is hard for people to decipher between murmuring and constructive concerns.

In our school, our leadership team members all support the Benedictine Values our institution was built on, but, at the same time, we did not want to have any prairie-dogging going on. We wanted our faculty to have the confidence to speak up and know they would be heard so that we could deal with problems as they occurred because we knew that if problems are not dealt with, they seldom go away and often become even bigger.

A phrase I use with my team to get this point across is, "*Make sure you deal with a problem or conflict when it is a pimple. If not, it will turn into a boil, and we will have to lance it.*" Although this analogy is a bit graphic, it has been effective in helping our leadership team understand the importance of dealing with conflict and problems rather than just hoping they go away. Our goal has always been to deal with problems when they are a pimple and not a boil, with the goal of dealing with it so effectively that we never have to deal with that problem or issue ever again.

Because of the failure of people to speak up at meetings, I often tell my leadership team to reflect not only on what is said in meetings but also on what is not said. The things that go unsaid are often what keep a group from operating effectively and dealing with the true issues at hand. We need to help our faculty feel safe and risk speaking up because the likelihood of building a *dynamic* organizational culture would be impossible if we had faculty who would not be willing to speak the truth.

As a leadership team, we developed an organizational and shared governance structure we believed would help our school eliminate most conflicts. We also knew conflict would inevitably occur because we are all human, but we believed strongly in the importance of finding the underlying cause of conflicts as quickly as possible. Although we knew most people like to avoid conflict, we also believe that conflict in an organization with a strong positive culture can be a catalyst for the development of stronger professional and trusting relationships.

Lastly, after reading the book *Love Works*, I listed direct quotes on our leadership principles poster from the book that I thought were important to remember if we were to lead our faculty effectively. Three quotes jumped off the page at me:

"As a leader's seniority increases, that leader should make fewer decisions."

"Create a culture where great people want to work."

"Leadership is a lonely business. When we rely only on our own perspective, we miss our blind spots. We do the best we can, but [if] we have nobody telling us the real truth, we will not improve over time."

These quotes really spoke to me. As a result, I decided to include them at the bottom of the framed leadership principles that are given to each of our leadership team members. To this day, I use them as my leadership compass. You may notice that these leadership principles are common sense and not rigidly specific, giving us flexibility in adapting them to almost any situation and with almost any person.

Bring Your Leadership Principles to Life

As Dean, I knew listing leadership principles on a poster would be meaningless if not lived and modeled by me and the leadership team. The leadership principles poster was a great start to building our dynamic organizational culture, but just putting them on a poster for us to read was not enough. They had to be lived by every member of our leadership team.

When I was a coach, I remember key phrases I used with my players to instill and communicate our team values and to help develop team chemistry. One such phrase was, *"Good players make their teammates better."*

I used this often with my players to stress the importance of each person on the team and the importance of helping each other get better. The use of keywords or phrases helps organizational members learn the culture and helps instill an understanding of what is important and valued in the organization. A consistent reminder of the values an organization shares is especially important in keeping the values alive.

My idea was to use our leadership team meetings, including our Coffee Break, to continually emphasize the leadership principles that would guide our decisions. Our meetings began, as most do at the University of Mary, with a prayer or reflection. I began to start each meeting with a leadership lesson or an article or book that focused on one of our team's leadership values.

I remember one in which I presented a reflection on an article by Rob Jenkins in the *Chronicle of Higher Education* titled '*Getting You to Trust Them.*'

Jenkins had been a small college basketball coach before entering academia. As a coach, Jenkins had questioned whether it was better to be liked or respected by your players, but as an academic administrator, he found out that the answer was neither one: *"The most important thing, by far, was for faculty members to trust me. Everything else was secondary."*

This article started an hour-long conversation on how we as the leadership team could build stronger, more trusting relationships with our faculty, the value of trust in dealing with conflict and the importance of trusting each other. It was a great learning experience for all of us.

These times for reflection have become a wonderful way for all of us to grow and learn from each other and to continue to live our leadership principles. They have also helped our team build trusting relationships with each other and have truly made us a stronger and more leadership-focused team.

Chapter 4 – Lessons Learned

It is important for leaders to have a good understanding of who they are and what they believe before they can effectively lead others.

It is important that leaders in your organization are guided by *'leadership principles'* that are lived by all the leaders in the organization.

The leadership principles used by a leader should not be specific and tie a leader's hands but general in nature so that a leader can use them and adapt them for every situation.

The leadership principles that guide a leader should be aligned with the organization's identity, values, and culture.

Your leadership principles will not only help you become a more effective leader but help your organization develop a *dynamic* organizational culture.

If you want to become an effective leader and want to build a *dynamic* organizational culture, then you need to get out of the way and let your people make the decisions for which they are responsible.

Chapter 5

Step 5 – Create an Identity

"Just as an individual has an identity, so too does an organization. That identity defines who the organization is and shapes how members behave. It is central to the experience of employees."

– Sheila Margolis

An organization's *'identity'* can have a positive effect on its culture, strategic planning, marketing, decision-making, and its members' ability to collaborate and communicate, as well as its members' commitment to the organization. Organizations whose members feel connected to the organization's identity tend to have members who are more dedicated and productive than organizations without a strong organizational identity.

Most scholars view organizational identity from a social constructionist perspective in that they see an organization's identity as the held beliefs of an organization's members as to what is distinctive about the organization and brings meaning to its members. As a result, effective organizational leaders will use their organization's identity in the development of strategic and marketing initiatives to distinguish themselves from other similar organizations.

This is particularly true in new organizations that are trying to distinguish themselves from other similar organizations. A strong, distinctive identity can be a competitive advantage for any organization because it clearly articulates who it is to those inside and outside of the organization and, like an organization's culture, is transmitted through members' collective stories and chosen words, which gives the organization its enduring distinctive trademarks.

In organizations with a strong identity, members can clearly and enthusiastically articulate who they are to each other as well as to those outside the organization. As a result, organizations with a strong identity are likely to attract people who believe in and connect with that identity, which in turn can increase its ability to attract and retain qualified candidates.

One example of a corporation with a strong organizational identity is Disney World. I have a friend whose family has taken a vacation each year to Disney World in Orlando, Florida. Disney World holds a special place in their hearts. Right after graduating from college, their son applied to work there. I asked my friend why his son wanted to work at Disney World. His reply was simply: *"Because it is 'the happiest place on earth.' Who would not want to work at Disney World?"* For my friend and his family, there was no better place on earth.

Disney World has always had a strong corporate identity and has continued to capture the attention of over seven hundred million people of all ages from around the world for the last 50 years. Most people would agree that Disney World's success and power lie in its brand positioning around happiness. Disney makes it all about the personal experience of its guests, and it tries to make people think of happiness when they think of Disney. Disney World's identity is clearly linked to its organizational culture and image and is a key element in its market brand as *'the happiest place on earth.'*

Organizational Values and Identity

For every strong organization, there is a direct connection between its values and its identity. An organization's culture and the values its members share can significantly impact member performance. Organizational members who feel personally aligned with their organization's identity are more likely to adopt its values and help make those values come to life.

At the University of Mary, we identify our identity in these words: *"We are faithfully Christian, joyfully Catholic, and gratefully Benedictine."* Based on the Benedictine heritage instilled by the Benedictine Sisters who founded the University of Mary in 1959, our organizational identity is alive and well and is our institution's major marketing tool and the focus of our strategic initiatives.

Our organizational identity is well understood by our community members at all levels, including staff, faculty, and students. Each of the schools on campus has a faculty representative on the Mission Integration Committee, which works to keep our identity and culture alive and well.

As I mentioned earlier, most meetings on campus begin with a reflection or prayer. In our school meetings, each faculty or staff member takes a turn giving a prayer or reflection. Likewise, most faculty at the University of Mary start their classes with a prayer or reflection and students often volunteer to give the prayer or reflection. It is our culture, our heritage, and our identity and lived by all of us in our community.

The Benedictine Sisters, who live at Annunciation Monastery on campus, are recognized at every event, and we are reminded frequently to be grateful for their work in founding and nourishing the University of Mary. In the past, Sisters often taught courses or held administrative positions in our institution. Although the Benedictine Sisters are fewer in number, they remain active in community events and activities and intentionally work to keep our Benedictine identity alive.

The Prioress of Annunciation Monastery, Sister Nicole Kunze, attends most university functions. In our school, our faculty often invite her to their classes to speak to students about our Benedictine heritage and share with our students who we are as a community. Sister Nicole is a symbol of who we are and the values we share as a community of learners, and she helps keep our Benedictine identity alive.

Because the graduate programs in our school are offered online, we understand that it is hard for these students to truly touch and feel who we are as a Christian, Catholic and Benedictine institution. As a result, we try our best to bring our graduate students to campus at least once for a summer residency so they can see, hear, and feel our Benedictine identity. At these summer residencies, Sister Nicole is invited to speak to our graduate students and give our graduate students a better understanding of our strong Benedictine heritage and identity. Our graduate students will often say that their summer residency is where our identity came to life for them and where they understood more clearly who we were as an institution.

A more formal event that helps our faculty remain connected to our Benedictine identity and heritage is the Sponsorship Formation Event that the Benedictine Sisters organize each year for leaders on our campus. The Sponsorship Formation Event is used to help our leaders develop a deeper commitment to the Christian, Catholic and Benedictine values that form our identity. The event includes a speaker, prayer, reflection, and time to build community with other leaders on campus. Each Sponsorship Formation Day ends with a song of blessing by the Benedictine Sisters, who surround us with raised hands to symbolize that they hold us in prayer every day.

The University of Mary formation events have significantly impacted my growth as a person and as a Dean. At one such event, the speaker talked about the importance of viewing our job or position as a vocation instead of a job or a career. She noted that the word *'vocation'* comes from Latin *'vocare,'* which means *'to call,'* and she challenged us to not be centered on our jobs, but on what we are being called to do. This Sponsorship Formation Day speaker helped me, and all attendees, better understand the role we play at the University and that we have been called to make a difference in the lives of our students.

Lastly, all faculty at the University of Mary participate in a Formation Day Retreat, with each school hosting its own retreat. When I was hired as Dean of our school, we held our school's first Formation Day Retreat in Medora, a tourist destination in western North Dakota. During the retreat, we grew together as a community and developed stronger relationships with each other. It was a wonderful time that gave all of us a better understanding of our institutional identity and a stronger connection to our institution and each other.

These Formation Retreats are held each year for our new faculty and staff during their first month of employment. New faculty and staff are required to attend this retreat and to engage in rigorous study and discussions about the Benedictine Wisdom Tradition and Catholic Intellectual Tradition. Although new community members often wonder why they need to participate in this retreat, after the event I often hear stories from our new community of how much they learned about the University of Mary, about our heritage and our identity as a Christian, Catholic and Benedictine university. They are always so grateful for the experience and come away as more committed and dedicated community members.

Our identity was built by our Benedictine Sisters, who remain living examples of our values, displaying respect, hospitality, and service to others within our community and to those in the broader community. As a result, when our faculty or others in our institution hear or see someone not acting in the spirit of our values, you might hear someone say, "*...that is not very Benedictine.*"

At the University of Mary, we all understand the value of our institutional identity. We know it is what connects us as individuals in our community and helps us in the work we do for our students, our academic programs and each other.

What Words Describe Who You Are?

When building an organizational identity, leaders should remember there are often autonomously operating *'subcultures'* that can affect the development of an organization's identity. These subcultures are formed by groups of people in the organization who share a communal problem or a unique experience. In higher education, these subcultures are most often formed by school, department, or program alignments.

These subcultures are more prevalent in new organizations that have not developed or established a strong identity. As new organizations develop, subcultures often come into play because each is struggling for its own identity. Bringing these subcultures together can be a challenging task for leaders in new organizations.

Knowing this, I tried my best as Dean to make sure our school's identity would integrate well with our institution's strong Benedictine identity. I knew the term *'community,'* one of our guiding Benedictine values, was often used to describe the members of the University of Mary.

As part of their monastic pledge, the Benedictine Sisters make a lifelong commitment to live together in the community with mutual respect, love, service, patience, and obedience, including communal discernment and decision-making. The Benedictine Sisters exemplify what it means to live in a community with their mutual concern, strong relationships, and commitment to each other.

As Dean, however, I wanted a different word - a unifying term - to describe our school faculty and staff, to mark what differentiated us. Organizational leaders often underestimate the power of the words they use to describe their organization or its members. How an organization's members view themselves and the words they use to describe themselves are significantly important in building a dynamic organizational culture. Words have a powerful effect on how members view and interact with each other.

The power of words can be illustrated in the names given to sports teams. I have a son-in-law who is from Iowa and he and his family are avid University of Iowa *'Hawkeye'* fans. He and his family members follow University of Iowa sports, but, primarily, the University of Iowa Hawkeye football. On game day, they fly a Hawkeye flag and wear Hawkeye sports gear. They live and die with the Hawkeyes.

I had an Associate Dean who is an avid Texas A&M *'Aggies'* football fan. She and her husband both graduated from Texas A&M, and she watches every Texas A&M football game and so do her family members. She, similar to my son-in-law, lives and dies with the success of their university's athletic teams and clearly identifies with her alma mater and its nickname.

In North Dakota, our two largest higher education institutions have strong institutional identities, the University of North *'Fighting Hawks'* and the North Dakota State University *'Bison.'* The University of North Dakota (UND) in Grand Forks is the largest university in the state, and since 1930, its sports teams have been known as the *'Fighting Sioux'*. Prior to 2012, the Fighting Sioux nickname and logo had clearly given the institution a unique and strong identity and was a source of pride. However, there were Native Americans and others in the state who saw the name as demeaning to Native Americans and their Native American culture.

The Fighting Sioux nickname and logo were cited by the NCAA as a hostile representation of Native Americans, and on June 14, 2012, the state Board of Higher Education voted to get rid of the UND's moniker and Indian head logo.

On November 18, 2015, UND President Robert Kelly announced a new nickname for the sports teams - the *'Fighting Hawks'*. The new logo was the profile of a hawk head over the letters ND. Unfortunately, the name change has not been well received by all of its alumni and its avid sports fans who believed UND had lost its sports identity with the change in its name and logo.

The reasons for dropping the Fighting Sioux name and logo may have been necessary and appropriate, but it clearly has had an impact on the institution's identity. UND will successfully transition to the '*Fighting Hawks*,' but from a public perspective the change in identity has been difficult. Because once an organization changes its identity, especially an organization with a strong institutional identity, like the University of North Dakota, only time will bring back that strong institutional identity UND had for a century.

The second largest higher education institution in our state is North Dakota State University (NDSU) and their sports teams are known as the '*Bison.*' NDSU's football team has had an unprecedented level of success. Since 2011, the NDSU football team has a record of 149-12 and has won nine NCAA Division I FCS National Championships, which makes them the most successful college football program in Division I FCS this decade. The NDSU football team is the Bison - proudly known as the '*Thundering Herd.*' To be a Bison has become a badge of honor and gives the institution a strong identity. You see NDSU football jerseys everywhere. NDSU football championship stickers are proudly displayed on vehicles across the state.

In addition to a sports team's name, my experiences as a college basketball coach also gave me a unique perspective on the value of having a team identity. I noticed most successful basketball teams had not only talented players and good coaches but most importantly, they had a team identity. Some basketball teams had an identity as high-scoring up-tempo teams and other basketball teams had an identity as ball control teams who made every possession count. These different playing styles were created by the coach's philosophy and what the coach believed to be the most successful style of play. As a coach, knowing the identity of the team we were going to face helped tremendously with game preparation and understanding what my players needed to do.

One example of this is the Syracuse University men's basketball team coached by Jim Boeheim who retired in 2023. The Syracuse University men's basketball team has won 10 Big East regular season championships, 5 Big East tournament championships, and 34 NCAA tournament appearances, including 5 Final Four appearances with 3 appearances in the national title game.

Any college basketball coach or fan could tell you the identity of the Syracuse University men's basketball team. If asked, they would tell you they are known for their *'2-3 zone defense'*. A 2-3 zone defense is something very few other college coaches do, but this was his team's defensive style, their identity as a team. As a result, he recruited players who would be successful with the 2-3 zone defense.

One evening, I was watching *'The Basketball Tournament (TBT)'* on ESPB, a single-elimination tournament with sixty-four teams from throughout America competing for the TBT title and a $1 million winner-take-all prize. The 2020 winner of the title and $1 million was *'Boeheim's Army'*, made up of Syracuse University alumni who played for Coach Boeheim.

As I watched the tournament, I wondered if Boeheim's Army would play a 2-3 zone defense. Sure enough, the first time they were on defense, they played a 2-3 zone defense and that is what they played throughout the tournament. Why? Because that is the defense a Syracuse University team is expected to play and who they are; it is their identity.

Boeheim's Army was a testament to the strong identity created at Syracuse University by Coach Boeheim. These alumni believed in the 2-3 zone defense as players at Syracuse University. They did not seem to care how other teams played defense; at Syracuse, we play a 2-3 zone defense, and we are proud of it.

Developing and Defining Your Identity

As in the above examples, it was vital for our school to have its own identity to describe who we were as an organization. I also knew these our identity and the values we shared based on our identity must be developed and lived by the leaders and the faculty in our school. Because of my coaching background, the word *'team'* came to mind. I had used the word team throughout my time as Chair and, as a Dean, to describe who we were, so I knew it would not be foreign to our faculty and staff. It appeared to resonate with our faculty and carried, I believed, the strong connotation that we are all in this together and each of us has a role to play to help us succeed. I knew a dedicated team would be needed if we were to achieve our Vision 2030 goals.

So, I decided to use the simple word **TEAM** as our identifier, a differentiator that clearly defined who we were. The word community accurately described who we were as an institution, but I wanted a term unique to our school. I have noticed that leaders often use the term *'family'* to describe their organizations identify. For me, however, family did not accurately portray who we were as a school, and for me the word family was both overused and misleading.

I agreed with Todd Henry, the author of *Herding Tigers: Be the Leader That Creative People Need*, who wrote:

"...I shudder when I hear a leader refer to a team or the company culture as 'family.' No, no, no. You are not family. Families are connected by blood or by bonds that can't be broken, and membership in a family is unconditional. However, membership in your organization requires the adoption of a certain set of behaviors and subscription to cultural ideals and norms. If at any point someone violates those norms, his connection to your team is subject to termination. It is misleading and maybe even a little manipulative to your team members to give them the impression that they are part of something like a family. It is

often insecurity on the part of a leader that leads to such sentiments."

As I reflected on the character, talents and skills of our faculty and a team identity that could create a *dynamic* school culture. I started by making a list of the team values, that is, the faculty traits, attitudes and personal attributes that would give us a distinctive team identity.

One weekend, I was watching a '*60 Minutes'* segment, '*How the Chicago Cubs finally won the World Series after 108 years.*' The segment focused on team president Theo Epstein and his plan to go '*from worst to first'* by drafting promising hitters and players with strong character.

The 60 Minutes segment included this exchange between interviewer Bill Whitaker and members of the Cubs organization:

Bill Whitaker: *"So you're looking for more than just their skills. You're looking for character."*

Theo Epstein: *"Yeah. Because baseball is a game with a ton of adversity inherent in it. And players that tend to respond to adversity the right way and triumph in the end are players with strong character. If you have enough guys like that in the clubhouse you have an edge on the other team."*

Whitaker: *"You said, 'I used to scoff at character.' What changed?"*

Epstein: *"I just saw over the years that the times that we did remarkable things, it was always because players didn't want to let each other down. Players wanted to lift each other up."*

Whitaker: *"So how do you determine which player has the character traits you're looking for?"*

Epstein: *"Find out how he treats people when no one's looking. You go talk to their girlfriend. You go talk to their ex-*

girlfriends. You go talk to their friends. You talk to their enemies."

The two then discussed Kyle Schwarber, who had been a promising young hitter at Indiana University and who had been interviewed by local scouts from various major league baseball teams. But for the Cubs, Epstein did the interview, then made Schwarber his top draft pick.

Whitaker: *"What was it about his character that impressed you?"*

Epstein: *"Kyle played baseball with a football mentality."*

Whitaker: *"What do you mean?"*

Epstein: *"He would run through a wall in order to catch a ball. He would attack any obstacle that faced the team."*

Disaster struck Schwarber in the first week of his second season - running flat out chasing a fly ball, he tore the ligaments in his knee so badly that doctors said he would be out for the entire season. Nevertheless, he attacked rehab relentlessly.

Kyle Schwarber: *"I wanted to challenge myself, and I wanted to get back as soon as possible."*

While Schwarber was rehabbing, the Cubs were dominating. The pressure kept building - pressure that could have crushed this young team. Manager Joe Maddon had the antidote.

Joe Maddon: *"I talked about pressure and expectations as being positives. Embrace it. Embrace the target. Embrace the pressure. Embrace expectations. Because if you do, you could end up winning the first World Series in 108 years in Chicago."*

Maddon came to the Cubs after managing in Tampa. Once, when Tampa got off to a terrible start, Maddon showed why everyone wanted to work for him.

Whitaker: *"Your team lost the first six games. And you're flying off to the seventh. And you go through the plane, and you pour a drink for each one of your players. And they have no idea why you're doing this."*

Maddon: *"I had this really good bottle of whiskey. Pour a little shot in each guy. And then I went up to the front, got the PA system and I announced, 'to the best 0-6 team in the history of Major League Baseball.'"*

Whitaker: *"So what was the lesson from that? What did that do?"*

Maddon: *"It's about never quitting. It's just to break the tension. So, the burden was lifted. Pressure eased. And I could play baseball again."*

Maddon puts his own motivational sayings on T-shirts which he gives to his players.

Whitaker: *"You have a favorite?"*

Joe Maddon: *"Try not to suck."*

Watching this, I thought we could do something similar in our school to help our school build an identity. My major questions I asked myself were: *"How do I do something like this in our school?"* and *"What will work for faculty in higher education?"*

I knew higher education faculty are uniquely different than professional athletes, yet I knew they were like most other human beings in that they wanted to be part of something bigger than themselves and have a true sense of belonging. As I thought about how to build our school's identity, I wanted to do something like what the Chicago Cubs did; something that would resonate with our faculty and give our school a unique team identity. We had built a talented team of faculty members but needed something to unite us and give us a strong school identity.

As I mentioned earlier, our leadership team has framed posters of our leadership values that they display in their office. It has worked well for our leadership team because the poster reminds us daily of the leadership values we share as a leadership team. As I reflected on ways to create our identity, I thought, why not do something similar with our faculty and create a framed poster of our team values and give this poster to each faculty member?

As I explored ways to create a team identity, my first thought was to develop an operational definition for the word *'team'* because the word team can mean different things to different people. I wanted to define the word team that was aligned with our efforts to create a dynamic organizational culture in our school.

For me, step one in this process was to simply read dictionary definitions of the word team. What I learned was that the word team was defined as:

- *A group of people who play a particular game or sport against another group of people.*
- *A group of people who perform interdependent tasks to work toward accomplishing a common mission or specific objective.*
- *A number of people associated together in work or activity.*

I reviewed these definitions and soon realized none of them truly operationally described the word *'team'* in a way that would resonate with our faculty. I then put pen to paper and instead of defining the term team, I listed the attributes of what it meant to be a team member in our school. I realized each of our faculty members would have their own personal definition for the word team, but I wanted them to think more about what it meant to be a team player in our *dynamic* organizational culture.

I wanted the words to highlight who we were as a team and what we wanted to see in ourselves, our leadership team members, and our faculty members. Just like the Cubs who wanted players with character, we needed faculty with character, who worked hard and who believed they could create their own destiny.

I chose the words carefully and tried to find words that represented what I saw in our leadership team, because I knew if these values were already being demonstrated by our leaders, it was more likely our school faculty would embrace these values, as well.

My final draft was: *"We dream big, work hard, do not fear failure, embrace challenges, do not make excuses, and we know we have the ability to create our own future. Why? Because we are a **TEAM** and believe in the trust each other."* For me, this accurately described who we were and what we expected from each other.

After defining our **TEAM** mantra was created, I had posters printed and I gave a copy to each faculty member at our school's strategic planning workshop. I did not share the poster with my leadership team or request their input because I wanted honest feedback from everyone.

The **TEAM** poster I had created is listed below:

UNIVERSITY of MARY

for Life.

Liffrig Family School of Education and Behavioral Sciences

We dream big, work hard, take risks, do not fear failure, embrace challenges, do not make excuses, and know we have the ability to create our own future!

Why?

We are a TEAM and we believe in and trust each other!"

At the end of the workshop, I showed the '*60 Minute's* segment about the Cubs to my faculty. I talked to them about the value of building a team and my belief that we had built something like the Cubs. I then passed out the framed posters and shared why these team values were important and my belief that each of our leadership team and faculty members already lived these values.

Below are the set of words that define us as a **TEAM**, followed by my own explanation of how I defined them and why I selected them.

- Dream big.

    "Believe in the impossible! We are going to dream big because we can do whatever we put our minds to. Why? We have the competent and dedicated faculty and if we work together anything will be possible."

- Work hard.

    "Do your job as best you can! Nothing is ever achieved without hard work, and I have watched all of you work and no faculty on our campus work harder than you all do."

- Take risks.

    "Do something that may not be successful! If we want to succeed, we need to take risks. I want you to feel free to take risks and to try anything you believe will help us develop the best academic programs on campus."

- Do not fear failure.

    "It is OK to fail because that is how we learn! I want you to know that you will never be criticized for trying something to make your programs better, even if it does not work. Failure will be our best teacher."

- Embrace challenges.

*"I want you to take on any obstacle you may face boldly! Why? Because we are going to face challenges as a **TEAM**, but together we will overcome these challenges."*

- Do not use excuses.

"An excuse is nothing more than giving yourself a reason to fail! We are not going to use excuses for our failures, but instead we will own our failures and then move on."

- And, Know we have the ability to create our own future!

*"It is not the President or anyone else who can create our future. It is us and us alone. However, as a **TEAM** we have the faculty needed to become whoever we want to become and create the future we want for us and our students."*

In the discussion that followed, our leadership team members passionately supported these values, and by the end of the meeting, all our faculty members were on board.

I told our faculty I would like to have each poster displayed in every faculty member's office as a reminder of who we were, what identifies us, but most importantly, what values define us as a **TEAM**. To this day, every faculty member at that meeting has this poster in their office. All new faculty are given the poster as part of the onboarding process. My poster sits on a shelf in my desk, as a visual reminder of what distinguishes us from other schools at the University of Mary.

My efforts to create a shared identity for our school integrated with our institution's identity have been transformational and given our school a unique, distinct identity. We are members of the Liffrig Family School of Education and Behavioral Sciences **TEAM** and are proud of it.

To keep our identity thriving, I intentionally use the words in the poster when talking to our faculty, so they are consistently reminded as to who we are, what we believe and the values we share. They would also need to be lived by our faculty and put into action if we wanted them to become part of our culture.

Building a *dynamic* organizational culture is only possible when people voluntarily agree to live our **TEAM** values and make it our school's identity. Our team values do that and have allowed our school to thrive and grow.

Continue to Build Your Identity

Our leadership team are important players because they lead our faculty daily. As I have mentioned previously in Chapter 4, at our monthly leadership team meetings, I personally give the prayer or reflection and intentionally use this time to continue to build our team identity and emphasize our leadership team values so our leaders understand the vital role they play in creating our school identity.

At one such meeting, I took the opportunity to share with my leadership team members an article I read in the *Harvard Business Review* article titled, '*Burnout at Work isn't just about Exhaustion. It's also about Loneliness.*' This article focused on how workplace exhaustion often leads to loneliness when employees feel isolated or lack social support at work. The authors of this article suggest that leaders can reduce employee loneliness by promoting a workplace culture of inclusion and empathy, encouraging employees throughout the organization to build networks and celebrate collective successes and work as a **TEAM**.

When problems arise, most leaders can often become overwhelmed. However, if we are a **TEAM**, we can better manage these situations and so can our faculty because we are in this together. No problem is owned by one person, but every problem is owned by all of us. We are a **TEAM** and together we can do anything we put our minds to.

As our leadership team members discussed this article, the conversation moved to how to help faculty with burnout by leading with patience and respect. We also discussed the need to continue to celebrate the achievements of our faculty, building strong relationships with our faculty and strengthening our leadership team by being good teammates.

These leadership meetings have been special for me and, I think, for our leadership team members; it has become a time for us to grow together. Most importantly, however, it is a time for us to continue to reflect on who we are and the school identity we want to create and to remind us, as leaders, of the key role we play in building a *dynamic* **TEAM** culture.

One method I use to determine if our **TEAM** identify is truly lived and coming to life is how often I see or hear our faculty use the word **TEAM** in their personal communications and interactions. At our school meetings I often hear faculty members referring to the faculty in their program area as being part of the *'psychology,' 'counseling'* or *'education'* **TEAM**. I rarely hear our faculty members use the term *'program'* or *'department'* faculty. Instead, they call their colleagues their teammates or team members.

Likewise, it is common for our faculty to use the word **TEAM** in their email correspondences when referring to faculty in their academic area. This might seem insignificant to people outside of our school, but for me when our **TEAM** identity comes to life through our faculty interactions, it means it is real and truly alive. Faculty members who feel part of a **TEAM** are more likely to take risks and dream big because they know they have the support of a **TEAM** behind them.

Chapter 5 – Lessons Learned

It is important that your organization has a strong distinctive '*identity*' that will clearly define who you are and what you value as an organization.

An organization's identity will not only help a leader attract people to the organization, but it will help retain them, as well.

If your organization has a strong identity, your members should be able to articulate in words what makes their organization distinctive or sets it apart from other similar organizations.

As a leader, never underestimate the '*power*' of the written '*word*' to describe who you are and what you believe in as an organization.

Do not underestimate the value and importance of a strong organizational identity in the development of a *dynamic* organizational culture. Why? Because an organization's culture and identity are connected and inseparable.

Chapter 6

Step 6 – Create a Shared-Governance Organizational Structure

"Organizational structure provides guidance to all employees by laying out the official reporting relationships that govern the workflow of the company."

– David Ingram

Most organizations are structured around an *'organizational chart'* that visually depicts an organization's structure and the various positions within it, along with roles, responsibilities, relationships, and lines of authority of each position in the organization. Organizational charts are usually created vertically, with positions ranked from top to bottom and provide a visual reminder to everyone in the organization as to who is responsible for what.

I have learned that an organizational chart can significantly influence an organization's culture and its members' job satisfaction and commitment. Why? How an organization is organized directly affects its members' view of the chain of command, the flow of authority and the communication structure that exists within the organization. All of which can hinder or help an organization function effectively.

Impact of an Organizational Structure

An organizational chart clearly outlines who has authority and power within the organization. Anyone viewing an organizational chart often assumes that the closer a position is to the top of the chart, the more power the person in that position has within the organization. This person's positional power is often described as *'legitimate power'* because it has been granted to people in a position based on the organizational structure of the organization. People in positions at the top of the organizational chart are seen as having the authority to give orders to those below them with subordinates often complying solely because of the legitimacy of that position.

Although legitimate power is based on a person's position on the organizational chart, *'referent power'* is given to leaders in an organization because of the admiration and respect followers have for the leader and, most often is a result of a leader's ability to inspire and influence others.

Although an organizational chart may formally outline who holds the legitimate power positions, it is sometimes far more important to understand who has referent power. Power does not come from a title alone; it also comes because of the trust followers have in a leader because of the leader's personal attributes.

Structure alone will not propel the organization forward; that comes from the people who are put in the organization's positions of authority. The best-run organizations put people in leadership positions who are true leaders of the organization, those who are respected. Therefore, great care must be taken in the selection of the people who are placed in an organization's leadership positions. A person may have legitimate power, but when people are asked to trust and sacrifice for a leader, the leader must also have referent power.

In his book, *The 21 Irrefutable Laws of Leadership: Follow Them and People Will Follow You,* John Maxwell states,

"When people respect you as a person, they admire you. When they respect you as a friend, they love you. When they respect you as a leader, they follow you."

Similarly, in his book, *Start with Why: How Great Leaders Inspire Everyone to Take Action,* Simon Sinek states:

"Being the leader means you hold the highest rank, either by earning good fortune or navigating internal politics. Leading, however, means that others willingly follow you—not because they have to, not because they are paid to, but because they want to."

So, it is important for leaders to understand the impact an organization's structure can have on its members. An organization's structure directly affects how decisions are made and who has the decision-making power. In most organizations, these decisions are made primarily by those who are in positions of authority based on their position in the organizational chart.

My past experiences have shown me that the most effective organizations do not rely solely on the decision-making ability of their leaders but also allow their members to be involved in the decision-making process. The literature on this topic provides evidence that organizational leaders who allow their members to become involved in the decision-making process will often have people who have a *'greater sense of belonging'* and a stronger *'commitment'* to the organization.

In addition, these organizations are more likely to have the ability to *'transfer knowledge,'* that is, share information or ideas more effectively across the organization, than those organizations where decisions are made primarily by those in legitimate power positions.

Knowledge transfer within any organization can significantly increase its efficiency and productivity. As a result, it is important to create organizational structures that foster member involvement, decision-making, and collaboration.

People who are trusted to make decisions are often more creative, innovative, and engaged. Those involved in decision-making feel more connected to the organization and, therefore, more willing to take risks and work harder to help the organization succeed.

Higher Education Organizational Structure

Most higher education institutions are structured with a governing board, usually called a board of trustees, a president, faculty and various administrative positions within their colleges or schools. Each college or school is led by a dean who is responsible for the recruitment, appointment and retention of academic administrators, faculty, and staff.

A chairperson or department head is usually assigned as the supervisor or leader of each department in the school or college. Faculty members are given the rank of professor, associate professor, assistant professor, or instructor.

Faculty are most often represented by an academic senate or similar organization of faculty representatives who assist in the internal governance and, more specifically, with the academic governance of the institution.

In higher education, this is most often referred to as a *'shared-governance'* structure. The shared-governance structure may vary from institution to institution, but it is how most colleges and universities function. It requires the institution's governing board, senior administrators, and faculty to participate together in the decision-making process and the development of institutional policies.

In theory, a shared-governance structure in higher education is designed to promote collaboration, accountability, and decision-making, giving ownership to the faculty who will be required to implement those decisions. However, as Dr. Brian Mitchell, past Bucknell University and Washington & Jefferson College points out, *"There is a natural tension among these groups that is meant to ensure a kind of checks-and-balances system to produce thoughtful outcomes."* This tension is most often caused by the need for higher education administrators and governing boards to make decisions quickly to respond to the ever-changing landscape of higher education.

This was evident during the Covid-19 pandemic when presidents in higher education often had to make tough decisions about closing their campuses, moving to remote learning platforms, and securing funding resources to keep their institution financially stable during the pandemic.

Although a shared-governance structure is common in higher education institutions, in higher education institutions, a *'top-down'* governance structure often becomes the reality, especially during challenging times, with senior administrators taking the primary responsibility for making the major institutional decisions and setting policies.

Pressure to respond and react to situations often means institutions need to make decisions quickly. As a result, the shared-governance structure is sometimes ignored because of the time and energy needed to involve key organizational stakeholders in the decision-making process.

In our school, we had administrative leaders and faculty that could make a shared-governance organizational structure work, but we all knew that it would take time and slow the decision-making process. However, I believed it would strengthen our *dynamic* organizational culture, but I must admit, I was anxious about such a structure because to achieve our Vision 2030 goals, our school would need the ability to adapt and change quickly.

As I reflected on how to do this, two quotes kept running through my head. One quote was from Joel Manby in his book *Love Works*, *"As a leader's seniority increases, that leader should make fewer decisions."*

The other quote was from Simon Sinek that I heard from a talk he had given, in which he stated:

"The people at the top have all the authority, but the people at the bottom have all the information. The goal is not to push the information up. The goal is to push the authority down."

As I thought about these quotes, I knew our faculty, the people on the front lines, had the knowledge and expertise needed to run their academic programs and what needed to be done to meet the needs of our students. We had the faculty needed to make a shared-governance structure work. By giving our faculty, the authority to make academic program decisions we would have a better chance of achieving our Vision 2030 goals because it would give ownership of our academic programs to our faculty.

Experience has taught me that even higher education institutions with a shared-governance structure often fail to push authority down. This is most often the result of the institution's organizational structure. Most higher education institutions hire administrators to do *'administrative'* work and faculty to do *'faculty'* work, with little integration of administrative and work responsibilities.

Before the University of Mary moved to a school organizational model, the academic programs used a departmental organizational structure with faculty workloads based primarily on teaching workloads, with additional workload units given for advising, service and scholarly work. Although this faculty workload model is common in most units in higher education, it was important to create a new vision of how a shared-governance organizational structure could work with each faculty member given workload units for administrative work.

As Dean, I pondered how we could better structure our school to support a shared governance model that would allow our school to leverage the talents and gifts of each faculty member. I wanted faculty who joined our team to own their programs to increase academic program quality and creativity.

The *dynamic* organizational culture we were trying to create would require our faculty to take on tasks and responsibilities not usually given to teaching faculty. As a result, we needed to create an organizational structure that would give faculty the autonomy and authority to own these tasks and responsibilities.

As Dean, I am required each year to submit an organizational chart to our Office of Academic Affairs. For years, I submitted an organization chart that showed faculty assigned to various administrative roles in our school, but it was often only on paper and not truly alive in practice.

Our leadership team and I first considered the challenges ahead of us. We knew the implementation of such an organizational structure could potentially create angst among our faculty members who were not hired as administrators. Like other higher education institutions, our faculty were primarily rewarded for teaching, service, and scholarly work, not for administrative work and, as in most higher education institutions, faculty who apply for rank and promotion are evaluated on their independent work and not for their ability to collaborate with others.

Creating these new administrative roles for faculty in our school meant our leadership team would need to get our faculty to buy into this new shared-governance structure by educating them on the benefits of such a structure. Our leadership team would also need to provide professional development to help our faculty develop the administrative and leadership skills they need in these new roles.

We believed, however, that we had hired faculty who had the skills to take on these additional responsibilities. It might take time, but in the long run, we believed a shared-governance structure would be supported by our faculty, allowing our school to revise, build and create academic programs that would best meet the needs of our students and our institution and, most importantly, help build the *dynamic* organization culture we needed to meet our Vision 2030 goals.

Our School's Organizational Structure

With faculty being given the authority for administration, creation, and revision of our academic programs, I knew my role as Dean would change. As a result, my leadership philosophy and style would also have to change. I would need to live with less control and authority because I would be giving these responsibilities to our leadership team members and our faculty.

However, I was ready for the change, so I spent time personally reflecting on how I could embrace this new role. Although I knew this was the right direction to go, I knew it was not going to be easy for me to let go. I knew I would have to own the failures and mistakes of the faculty who would be placed in these new roles and that all the credit for future successes would need to go to the faculty.

I knew I was going to need to develop a leader-leader mindset. My major focus as the Dean would be to find and develop academic leaders who could administer, create, and strengthen our academic programs. With the growth of our academic programs and the increase in student enrollment, I knew I no longer had the expertise and knowledge to lead our school's academic programs.

As I pondered the need for a new leader-leader mindset, I also considered my limitations as a leader and whether I truly was a strong enough leader to pull this off. A quote from Simon Sinek gave me hope:

"The great leaders are not the strongest, they are the ones who are honest about their weaknesses. The great leaders are not the smartest; they are the ones who admit how much they don't know. The great leaders can't do everything; they are the ones who look to others to help them. Great leaders don't see themselves as great; they see themselves as human."

During the next few years, I reminded myself of this quote often. Together with my leadership team, we worked to create our school's new organizational chart. Our school had a chart in place documenting the administrative positions and lines of authority, but it did not truly represent the structure needed for us to move forward with the school initiatives we were focusing on.

The major initiative at the time was the development of an Education Doctorate (Ed.D.). We had just gone through an initial Higher Learning Commission (HLC) visit and had submitted our Interim HLC Report. Based on the feedback we received from the HLC visitation team, we knew we needed to first build an organizational structure that would allow us to effectively manage the graduate programs we currently had and our new Ed.D. program.

After discussing this issue with our school's leadership team, I proposed the creation of an Associate Dean position to oversee our growing graduate programs, with a Chair assigned to oversee our graduate programs.

I knew that if our graduate programs were to thrive, we would need to create an organizational structure that would allow our graduate programs the autonomy needed to grow and improve, and we would need a strong lead administrator in charge of each of these programs. In addition, our school was given the responsibility for the development of an Ed.D. Program in our school and finding a strong leader, as Associate Dean, was vital in making the addition of an Ed.D. Program a reality.

The first step I took was to meet with Dr. Carmelita Lamb, our Chair of Graduate and Distance Education and Dr. Brenda Tufte, our Chair of the Department of Education, both of whom were key members of our leadership team and faculty with high amount of referent power. These two highly respected faculty members had the passion, drive, vision, and leadership skills needed to make the Ed.D. a reality.

In the meeting, I asked Dr. Lamb to become the Associate Dean of our graduate programs and for Dr. Tufte to become the Chair of our Graduate Education Program. Without hesitation, both Dr. Lamb and Dr. Tufte eagerly and passionately agreed to take on these new leadership roles in our school. With these two on board, my leadership team and I met to discuss various organizational structures and how we could build a new shared-governance structure that would help us build our *dynamic* organizational culture.

We did not want an organizational chart or a shared-governance structure that only looked good on paper. We wanted leaders in these positions, not administrators who just followed orders from above. We wanted leaders willing to take risks, and dream big, with the courage and passion to build something special.

One item we discussed was allowing faculty to teach at both the undergraduate and graduate levels. In most institutions, faculty are given graduate or undergraduate rank status, with teaching responsibilities assigned accordingly. A combination of undergraduate and graduate teaching responsibilities is rare. We believed, however, that allowing our faculty to teach at both the undergraduate and graduate levels would foster interaction of both undergraduate and graduate faculty members, another step in building a *dynamic* organizational culture.

Most graduate faculty are required to have a doctoral degree in an appropriate discipline, along with demonstrated effectiveness in teaching and a record of productive scholarship. We had faculty in both undergraduate and graduate programs who met that degree criterion. So, we moved ahead, allowing faculty to be given both undergraduate and graduate faculty status and to give them both undergraduate and graduate teaching assignments.

The first organization chart we drafted included five administrative positions that would make up our school's leadership team. The five leadership positions included an Associate Dean of Graduate Programs to lead our graduate programs. In the undergraduate program, we created two leadership positions: the Chair of the Department of Education and the Chair of the Department of Behavioral Sciences. I knew we needed strong leaders in these positions who could collaborate and work closely together.

I presented our new organizational structure to the Vice President of Academic Affairs, who supported this new structure. We then presented our new organizational chart to the President's Council, which presented it to our Board of Trustees for approval.

As our school grew, we continued to add new administrative positions, including chair, program director and program coordinator administrative positions in both undergraduate and graduate programs. Adding these administrative positions allowed our school to move the decisions for academic programs down to the program level, with faculty in those programs having the authority to make the decisions needed to improve their programs and meet the needs of their students.

The faculty members in the chair positions are personally responsible for the supervision of their assigned program director and/or program coordinator and the development of their position descriptions and have become our academic leaders. They are expected to supervise and evaluate the program directors and coordinators in their academic areas. The chairs, along with their program directors and coordinators, own their academic programs and are held accountable for the development of strong student-centered academic programs.

Faculty Workload

With our school's organizational structure in place, the only task remaining for our leadership team was how to assign faculty workload units for each of the administrative positions in our organizational chart. Administrative workload units had always been given for faculty members in chair positions in our school but not for program directors or coordinators. Additionally, we were not given any new faculty positions for these administrative positions; therefore, we decided to distribute the administrative workloads among the faculty placed in administrative roles.

To make this happen, all our leadership team members, including me, would need to take on teaching responsibilities. It was clear we were all in this together, and to make this work, our faculty members would have to be given administrative roles and workload assignments for these administrative positions. They would also need to become not just administrators but effective leaders if we were to make this structure work and create the shared governance we had envisioned.

As I reflected on how to determine faculty workload that would reflect the administrative work, we were now asking faculty to do, I remembered a presentation at a Higher Learning Commission conference given by Dr. Rick Gillman, Associate Provost, and Dr. Jon Kilpinen, Dean of Arts and Sciences, at Valparaiso University.

Their presentation was titled, '*Creating Holistic Departments to Manage Faculty Workload*,' focused on supporting and rewarding faculty for doing differentiated work to fill institutional and departmental goals beyond the expectations of teaching and scholarship. Dr. Gillman and Dr. Kilpinen suggested we should view faculty as an "*Organic whole, not just a collection of talented specialists.*" They used a holistic approach to better leverage the diverse talents and skills of faculty and empower academic units to achieve their goals.

Their presentation churned up thoughts in my head as to whether a holistic workload model would work in our school. I began to envision how our school could use this '*holistic faculty workload*' concept to give workload credits to each faculty member for teaching, advising, scholarship and administrative duties. This type of faculty workload model was intriguing to me because I knew we had faculty who had the leadership skills needed to take on the administrative responsibilities of our school, but we did not have a way to use their leadership talents and skills effectively.

I knew our new organizational structure would allow our leadership team to push authority down to faculty who were doing the daily academic work. It would also help us become more efficient and would give the faculty the opportunity to use their academic expertise, leadership skills and teaching skills to the fullest.

Dr. Lamb and Dr. Tufte supported the idea, as did the other members of our leadership team. We then began to restructure our faculty workload policy to include the assignment of units for administrative work. We proceeded to discuss our ideas with the Assistant Vice President of Academic Affairs, Dr. Kim Long. Dr. Long had created a form that calculated the workload for faculty with units given for teaching and advising. We used this as a template, adding a section for assigning workload for administrative positions and, as a result, we created our school's first faculty holistic workload policy.

Today, all of the faculty members in our school have been assigned an administrative role. Workload units are given to each faculty member based on their administrative assignment. Our current administrative positions include chairs, program directors and program coordinators. Each of these administrative positions is assigned a set number of workload units, with an increase in workload units for each position based on the following department/program criteria: graduate or undergraduate, accreditation requirements, site supervision responsibilities, number of programs, number of fulltime, part-time, and adjunct faculty, number of students and number of credits generated.

Additional workload units are provided for faculty who supervise larger academic programs and programs that include clinical site supervision. Our workload policy allows all our faculty to be involved in decisions that affect their programs and gives our school the ability to innovate and change quickly and to continue to develop our dynamic organizational culture.

Our school's workload policy is the major component of our shared-governance organizational structure and truly allows decisions to be made at the program level. Our workload policy gives authority and responsibility for program quality and student enrollment to the faculty in our academic programs. These are the faculty who interact with our students and who know best what is needed to improve our programs.

A tremendous amount of work and time was put in, not only by me but our leadership team in the creation of our school's organizational structure and faculty workload policy, but it has all been worth it. It has allowed our school to grow and has truly been the major reason we have been able to develop the *dynamic* organizational culture we are living in today. In addition, it has given me more time as Dean to take responsibility for leading new initiatives and removing the barriers that prevent our academic programs from growing and improving.

Chapter 6 – Lessons Learned

Most organizational charts identify who has the *'authority'* and *'power'* in the organization; more importantly, an organizational chart should identify who are the leaders in the organization - the people others have chosen to follow.

To make an organization more effective, organizations need to create an organizational structure that leverages the talents and gifts of each person in the organization.

Never forget that an organizational chart is worthless if the people assigned leadership roles are not given the authority and responsibility to lead.

A *dynamic* organizational culture will not happen if a *'shared-governance'* organizational structure is not created that allows members of the organization to become part of the *'decision-making'* process.

As a leader in a shared-governance structure, it is often difficult to let go of the decision-making process, because you are still ultimately responsible for all decisions made by the faculty in your organization. Let go anyway!

The key leaders in any organization who are put in a power position must be people who have the talent, gifts, and drive needed to effectively *'lead'* and *'inspire'* others.

When defining the positions within an organization, a leader must try to give everyone a position of authority or responsibility to help make everyone feel like a valuable member of the organization.

Chapter 7

Step 7 – Avoid the "Manager Black Hole"

"Management is about persuading people to do things they do not want to do, while leadership is about inspiring people to do things, they never thought they could."

– Steve Jobs

After reading this quote from Steve Jobs, it gave me a new perspective on the difference between being a *'leader'* and being a *'manager.'* Even though all leaders must also be managers, leading is much different than managing and requires a much different skill set. I have known people in leadership positions who were great managers but during my career, I have had the opportunity to be led by only a few people who I would consider to be great leaders. Great leaders are hard to find because they have special talents and a mindset that is much different than that of a manager. If you have ever been in an organization led by a great leader, consider yourself fortunate because most people never have such an opportunity.

Warren Bennis, author of *On Becoming a Leader,* views leaders and managers as two distinctly distinct roles, managers being people who *"do things right"* and leaders as people who *"do the right thing."* When I became a Dean, I tried to remind myself of Bennis' definition of a leader and take the time to *'lead'* and not just focus my time and energy on my managerial responsibilities.

Unfortunately, I am like most organizational leaders who have a never-ending list of managerial tasks and responsibilities to tackle each day. I could spend every day on budget administration, hiring, development and assessing employee performance, strategic planning, developing organizational policies and procedures and other managerial tasks.

It is so easy for organizational leaders to become addicted to getting things done and measuring their effectiveness by the number of tasks they have accomplished each day or items on their do-to-do list they were able to check off. The responsibilities of being a manager can often be measured or at least identified and, as a result, can unconsciously give an organizational leader the impression they are doing their job.

On the other hand, the responsibilities and tasks of a leader often cannot be easily measured or identified. For example, an effective leader must continually inspire their followers to higher levels of performance and take time to build meaningful relationships with their followers. Yet, it is almost impossible to measure or evaluate any of these leadership skills. As a result, leaders often become focused on the things that they can see or measure and, as a result, spend their time on managing not leading.

An organizational leader's workday never ends and as a result, leaders can often fall into what I call the '*manager black hole.*' So many decisions need to be made and so many tasks need to get done, that out of necessity, leaders tend to unconsciously focus their time and energy on managing their daily tasks and often move from crisis to crisis or problem to problem rather than using their time to lead.

Organizational leaders who fall into the manager black hole often become leaders who have people who choose to work for them but have not made the personal decision to follow them. Organizational leaders who rarely find the time or energy to lead will never be able to create a *dynamic* organizational culture where innovation thrives and where people are willing to change and improve. Building a *dynamic* culture takes time and energy and rarely occurs without strong focused leaders who understand the importance of leading and who consciously avoid falling into the manager black hole.

Both leaders and managers need to have effective communication and organizational skills, but being a leader does require a person to have more complex skills. The chart below illustrates the differences I have found in the literature that defines the difference between being a LEADER and being a MANAGER.

LEADER	MANAGER
Does the Right Things	*Does Things Right*
Takes Risks	*Minimizes Risk*
Innovates	*Administers*
Inspires Trust	*Relies on Control*
Challenges Status Quo	*Accepts Status Quo*
Visionary	*Rational*
Asks What and Why	*Asks How and When*
Builds Teams	*Establishes Rules and Procedures*
Looks Outward	*Looks Inward*
Trusts and Develops	*Directs & Coordinates*
Creates Change	*Manages Change*
Uses Influence	*Uses Authority*
Uses Conflict to Improve	*Avoids Conflict*
Builds Teams	*Builds Consensus*
Create Circles of Influence	*Create Circles of Power*

To be a leader requires taking time to inspire, empower and motivate others. As Charles S. Lauer is quoted as saying, "*True leaders do not force people to follow; they invite them on a journey.*" Leaders must find the time to build meaningful professional relationships with those they serve and to build teams that create the change needed to move the organization from a static organizational culture to a *dynamic* organizational culture.

Leader-First Mindset

I believe a leader who wants to build a *dynamic* organizational culture must learn to develop a leader-first mindset, that is, they must view their primary role as a leader rather than as a manager. They must learn how to focus their energy and time on communicating a vision, inspiring others, and not solely on getting things done.

Managers can often be short-sighted, spending their time and energy on what they can manage and control. This can be rewarding and addictive because things that can be managed and controlled are usually things that can be measured. Managerial responsibilities are usually things that can be seen and, as a result, allow the leader to see progress with their own eyes.

On the other hand, a leader with a leader-first mindset spends their time on things that are not measurable, such as building trust, instilling confidence in others and motivating others. Leaders with a leader-first mindset spend their time doing things that do not necessarily bring immediate results.

As a leader, I personally believe in the *Eisenhower Principle*, which comes from the words of former President Dwight D. Eisenhower, who said: *"I have two kinds of problems, the urgent and the important. The urgent are not important, and the important are never urgent."*

I use the Eisenhower Principle to remind myself as Dean, that I will always run into problems or situations that require my urgent attention, but these problems should never cause me to forget my most vital role of leading others. My time should be spent on my most important responsibility, which is to build strong teams and relationships, instead of spending my time on problems that demand my immediate attention.

Urgent problems will always be part of any leader's day. This can make leaders lose their focus because the consequences of not dealing with urgent problems can have a significant negative impact on the organization. Nevertheless, it is important for leaders to not let the urgent overcome the important, or the leader will fall into the manager black hole. If a leader develops a leader-first, instead of a manager-first mindset, they will be more likely to able to effectively deal with the problems they encounter.

Are You a Leader or a Manager?

At a North Dakota Council of Educational Leaders conference, I gave a presentation titled, *How to Build and Develop a Team Culture*. During the presentation, I emphasized the importance of not falling into the manager black hole. At the end of the presentation, a school administrator asked me how he could tell if he was a leader or a manager.

My response was, *"It is actually quite easy to tell if you are a manager or a leader because how you spend your time will tell you if you are a leader or a manager."* I told him to write down on paper everything he did each day for two weeks. At the end of the two weeks, I asked him to note every activity on his list that included a conversation or an interaction with a teacher or staff member and to list these activities as leader activities.

Next, I told him to list any activity on his list that included no interaction with a teacher or staff member and to list these activities as manager activities. If, at the end of the two weeks, you have more leader activities than manager activities, you are a leader. However, if you have more manager activities than leader activities, you are a manager.

I know this simple exercise is not a research-based valid assessment of identifying managers from leaders, but it does help leaders determine where they spend their time. Managers tend to spend their time accomplishing tasks and leaders tend to spend their time interacting with people and inspiring and helping others do their job.

If you want to be a leader, you cannot spend your time sitting in your office completing paperwork or working on spreadsheets. A true organizational leader enjoys spending time with others and getting to know people on a personal level. Leading requires building trusting relationships with your followers. Unfortunately, building relationships takes time and cannot be done in isolation while sitting in an office where you spend your time documenting what you value. If you value getting things done, you are a manager; if you value spending time with others, you are a leader.

If you have read any books or articles about leadership or management, you will have more than likely seen the acronym MBWA, which stands for '*Managing By Wandering Around*.' MBWA does not imply a leader should just aimlessly wander around but outlines a legitimate strategy a leader can use to stay abreast of what is happening in the organization.

Leaders who believe in MBWA physically walk around their organization for the purpose of engaging with their followers to get a first-hand understanding of what is happening in their organization. To make this better fit my own personal leadership philosophy I use the term '*Leading*,' instead of '*Managing*' so I use the acronym LBWA (Leading By Wandering Around) to describe this leadership technique.

In the movie *The Darkest Hour*, Winston Churchill, the newly appointed British Prime Minister, must decide how to deal with the Nazi threat of invasion of Britain during World War II. His decision came down to negotiating with Hitler or fighting on, even when the hope of victory seemed impossible.

The movie depicts Churchill showing up in the London Underground, talking to ordinary people about whether to fight or negotiate. It was well known that Churchill would go AWOL, showing up in different areas of London to visit with ordinary people. Whether or not the Underground scene in the movie is factually true, it illustrates the value of leaders listening and getting into the trenches with their followers to learn what they believe and feel.

This scene in the movie is credited with Churchill's decision to fight on regardless of the cost, and the famous speech in which he says, "*We shall fight on the beaches, we shall fight on the landing grounds, we shall fight in the fields and in the streets, we shall fight in the hills; we shall never surrender...*"

I use LBWA to keep my finger on the pulse of the school by simply getting out of my office and visiting with my faculty. I might just drop into their office and ask how their classes are going or an initiative they had been working on.

Most faculty want their leaders to feel the work they do is important. Talking to my faculty about their work helps me better understand what they do and gives me insight into how they are doing and the issues they deal with as an instructor or administrator.

There are days when I have been at my desk for hours and must intentionally say to myself, "*Stop being a manager and lead. Visit with someone to see what is going on.*" It is so easy to just sit at my desk and focus on my managerial tasks, but I truly try to remember that the work at my desk, although important, is not my real job. My real job is to help my faculty to understand that I know their work is important and I value the work that they do. At these times, I often put my tasks aside and just get up and go somewhere, even just to pass by a faculty meeting or greet students in the hallway.

Seeing is believing. When members of any organization see their leaders, it makes them feel more connected to their leader and the impression their leader cares and is in the trenches with them. LBWA is useful for staying abreast of people's work, interests and ideas and can have a remarkable effect on the members of any organization. It might seem to be a gimmick, but if a leader does use LBWA and honestly listens to others, they will become better leaders, not falling into the manager black hole.

I also use LBWA weekly to get out of the office and talk to others on campus. My office is in the Benedictine Center, which also holds the business office, human resources, admissions, creative services, public affairs, student development and academic affairs. I spend time each week talking to people in these departments.

One day during my walk I ran into one of our graduate assistants who asked why she often sees me walking the halls of the Benedictine Center. I told her I was talking to people outside of my academic areas to develop relationships with those who affect my ability to do my job.

The graduate assistant seemed puzzled and then asked, *"So, you just wander around without a real plan of meeting anyone in particular?"* I said, *"Exactly, and the great thing about it is, I often run into the most important people on campus: our custodians, our plant services people, and administrative assistants."*

She then said, *"Why do you call them the most important people?"* I responded, *"Because they are in the trenches and often know more about what is going on than anyone else on campus. You would be surprised at what I learn from these people. Besides, I never know when I am going to need their help, so getting to know them as people can only help me do my job."*

My weekly networking trips keep me in the loop and allow me to develop connections with those in our community. As I have mentioned earlier in this book, I often remind my leadership team members, *"People don't trust people they do not know."* My LBWA leadership method has helped me build trusting relationships with people on campus.

One specific example of how my LBWA has served our school well is the relationships I have developed with our undergraduate and graduate admissions staff members. No one needs to tell me the importance of enrollment to our school and our university; I check our student enrollment dashboard each day to see how we are doing.

Our school's admissions representatives are truly the ones who make the difference in student recruitment efforts, so I try to visit them regularly to let them know I value the work they do and understand the tough job they have. One of our school's key admissions representatives is our graduate admissions coordinator. Our graduate admissions coordinator holds an extremely critical position because she is usually the first point of contact with prospective graduate students.

Each week I intentionally pass by our graduate admissions office just to talk and see if she is dealing with any difficult recruiting issues and to get a real-time assessment of how our graduate student recruitment is going. Often, I will suggest to her that we take a walk to talk so I can get a deeper understanding of the recruiting barriers she is facing and ideas of how to improve our recruitment efforts or academic programs. The time I spend visiting with her gives me a more accurate perspective or picture of our graduate recruitment efforts and has often provided the impetus needed to start different graduate enrollment initiatives.

In addition to visiting with our graduate admissions coordinator, I regularly stop by the office of undergraduate admissions and chat with our undergraduate admissions representatives. Our undergraduate admissions staff members are young professionals who often are in their first professional position. Yet, I have found they are full of energy and eager to succeed. I do my best to show my appreciation for the work they do and try to let them know that I consider each of them to be key members of our school team.

I remember on one of these visits, I stopped by one of our undergraduate admissions representatives just to say hi and check in with her. During this visit, she indicated how badly she was trying to get a psychology student accepted to the University of Mary and how frustrated she was because the student and her family had a strong connection to our university. She indicated that because of one low test score, the student's application was forwarded to our Academic

Standards Committee, which determines the fate of students who do not meet our academic standards.

I gave her ideas on how to present a case for admission for this student and as a member of the Academic Standards Committee, told her I would be willing to advocate for this student. As a result of this admissions representative's efforts and ability to present a convincing case as to why this student should be admitted, the student was admitted to the University of Mary. Our admissions representative was elated and thanked me for my support. I told her we were on the same team and that if she ever needed help again just stop by my office. As a result, our professional relationship grew, and she became even more committed to helping our school reach its enrollment goals.

One last example of the impact of my LBWA: on my daily walks I usually pass by the business office service desk window. I intentionally try to take time to say hi to one of the purchase clerks whose office is just inside the business office and near the reception desk. At the time, she had been at the University of Mary for less than a year and I wanted her to feel welcomed, so every time I would walk by the office, I would say *"Hi."*

As I mentioned, she was a purchasing clerk who works with purchase orders, and we had just moved to a new electronic format that required somewhat of a learning curve to navigate. When using our new online purchase ordering system, I inadvertently made a submission error, and I had to work with her directly to get it corrected. When other faculty made similar errors, she would politely request that they resubmit their purchase orders. However, with me she corrected my error and resubmitted the purchase order for me. I never asked her why she was willing to help me, but I know saying hi to her each day, as simple as it may be, did not hurt and it helped me develop a stronger personal and professional connection with her.

Taking the time to build these relationships with others on campus has directly impacted my ability to do my job and has opened my eyes to the work that others do to make the organization succeed. However, in today's digital age, you might think LBWA is an old management or leadership practice. Today, LBWA may not be solely a physical exercise, because the workplace has changed.

In our school, we now have three graduate counseling faculty who work remotely so I cannot physically meet with them each week. So, what I do is find the time to connect with these faculty each month to see how they are doing and just to help them feel part of the team. They are not physically in our building, but they are still key members of our team and, as a result, I want them to feel part of our team and our community.

Leaders Know Their Product

The Profit is a reality-based television program starring Marcus Lemonis, the founder, chair and CEO of Camping World/Good Sam, a national retailer of recreational vehicles and related goods and services. In this reality show, Lemonis invests his own money in small businesses that are struggling but businesses he believes have the potential to become successful. Dealing with these struggling businesses, Lemonis focuses on what he calls the three '*P*' components to help businesses become succeed. The three '*Ps*' are *people, products,* and *processes.*

In the episodes I have watched, one of the three P components is usually not working well; and sometimes all three need to be fixed. As I watched various episodes, I realized that in higher education, people, products, and processes are also extremely important. Much the same as a business, we need qualified people or faculty who have the knowledge, skills and attitude needed to meet the needs of our students; we need the correct processes in place in the development of courses, course sequencing, program budgeting, faculty evaluation, and program/student assessments; and we need to produce a product that attracts students and that gives our students the knowledge, skills and attitudes needed to become strong professionals.

In my time as a Dean, I can honestly say my emphasis on the value of people has never really changed, but my thoughts about process and product sure have. As a program director and department chair, I spent my time focusing on getting the processes right, which usually meant developing policies and procedures. Over time, however, as more faculty leaders were hired and my leadership team took ownership of these processes, I became more focused on our product and less process.

In higher education, our product is student learning, more importantly, the success of our students that is primarily affected by the performance of our faculty. Although the processes developed to help us develop our product are important, I know my main job as Dean is to instill a culture where our faculty took personal responsibility for student learning and the success of our graduates.

As Sister Thomas was fond of saying, *"At the University of Mary we measure our success based on the success of our students."* I have never forgotten the legacy she left and the value she put on meeting the needs of our students, which in her mind was job number one for administrators, faculty members and staff.

As I mentioned in Chapter 4, I often remind our leadership team to remember to *'look under the hood'*. to see if the engine is running smoothly. The only way for me to get a good understanding of how things are going is to review program data and talk to students and faculty. Although I do not expect our team members to know everything, I do expect them to be able to tell me how their academic programs are doing in terms of enrollment, faculty performance and program quality.

In the reality show *Shark Tank*, entrepreneurs present their business plans to a panel of five successful business executives - the *'sharks'* - who decide whether to invest in the company. The following six people are on the panel most frequently:

- *Barbara Corcoran*, a businessperson, investor, speaker, consultant, syndicated columnist, author, and television personality, and founder of The Corcoran Group, a real estate brokerage in New York City, which she sold to NRT for $66 million in 2001.

- *Mark Cuban*, an American entrepreneur, television personality, and media proprietor with an estimated net worth of $4.3 billion.

- *Lori Greine*, an American television personality, inventor, and entrepreneur known as *'the Queen of QVC.'*

- *Robert Herjavec*, Canadian businessperson, investor, television personality and founder of BRAK Systems, a Canadian integrator of Internet security software, was sold to AT&T Canada in 2000 for $30.2 million.

- *Daymond John*, an American businessperson, investor, television personality, author, motivational speaker, and founder, president, and CEO of FUBU.

- *Kevin O'Leary*, a Canadian businessperson, author, politician, and television personality and co-founder of SoftKey Software Products, a technology company.

These panel members will ask these aspiring entrepreneurs questions about their business, such as:

"What are your sales? How much debt do you have?"

"If we give you money, what will you do with the money?"

"What are your costs? What is the retail cost of your product?"

With these questions, these sharks are essentially *'looking under the hood.'*

If the entrepreneur cannot give solid, accurate information about their business, the sharks will say they are '*out*' - not interested, because the entrepreneur does not know their numbers.

As a Dean, I often feel like one of the entrepreneurs on Shark Tank. My president and vice-president of academic affairs expect me to have a good understanding of my product, that is, the academic programs in our school. This is most evident each fall semester when Deans are required to give a budget presentation to the President's Council, which includes the University of Mary President, Executive Vice President, and the Vice Presidents for Academic Affairs, Student Development, Financial Affairs, and Public Affairs.

At the Deans' budget meetings, each Dean gives a presentation focusing on the school's budget, student enrollment, program revenue and an analysis of the needs of the school, with an emphasis on any new faculty positions needed for the following year. In preparation for this meeting, I spent a tremendous amount of time going over our school's enrollment, tuition revenue and budget numbers. It is my responsibility to know everything about its academic programs and provide justification for any new school expenditures, especially when requesting new faculty positions.

At this meeting, each Dean had better know their numbers if they expect to be granted new faculty positions. I personally enjoy preparing and giving the budget presentation for my school because I have taken the time to personally review our academic program data, regarding enrollment, credit hours generated by program, and net revenue. I am always confident walking into this meeting because I know our school's product well and am ready to answer any question I am asked.

In my 12 years as Dean, I have been given almost all of the faculty positions requested. Why? Because I know my product, I know my numbers and I have been able to clearly articulate how the requested faculty position will impact our school's student enrollment and, bottom line, our net revenue. Also, I have never asked for a faculty position unless I can justify the position and document with real numbers how it will positively affect our school's ability to meet its enrollment and revenue goals.

In this meeting, I have never developed a PowerPoint or presented our school's information in an electronic format. Instead, I give the President's Council hard copies of my presentation that contain all the data needed to show how our school has performed and justification for the need for the requested faculty position.

I try not to give too much information because often that will only lead people into the weeds, but I try to present information in a format that is easy to read and sequential. Before I create the materials for my presentation, I always remind myself to keep it simple. Why? Because I want my presentation data to be easy to follow and in a format our President's Council members can easily understand.

Our President's Council members are smart, dedicated and committed people, but they do not know my school like I do, so I want to present our school data in a clear and concise manner. Giving them too much information can be overwhelming and get the discussion off target. I give them printed copies of my presentation so I can refer to selected pages, which allows them to view the data for themselves rather than trying to remember what I am telling them.

I purposely try to keep my presentation to less than 20 minutes because I know if they have questions, they will ask me. I am often teased by the other Deans that my presentation takes so long. And do you know what, it does, but not because of me, but because of questions from the President's Council members. As they review the data from my school, they often ask questions about the data or clarification questions so they can accurately interpret the data. With the President's Council members, I try to focus on the product and not the process because they do not care about the process. They just want to know the product, and that is what I give them.

I expect the same from my leadership team members who hold associate dean or chair positions in our school. I expect them to review their academic programs and student assessment data, enrollment numbers, retention numbers, and faculty evaluations so they have a good understanding of the quality of our product.

My leadership team members have access to dashboards that give them student enrollment and retention reports, academic program revenue reports, and student assessment data, so I expect them to be able to know the strengths, weaknesses, and needs of their academic programs. I expect our leadership team members, however, to not just rely on data or student assessment reports, but to spend time in faculty offices asking questions about our students and our academic programs.

I want our leadership team members to know our academic programs and faculty well. They can only do this by spending time with their faculty and their students, so they truly have a good grasp on how our students and academic programs are doing.

If a faculty member is not performing well or a student is thinking of dropping out, I expect our leadership team members to know this before it is too late. I want them to be leaders who focus on developing and improving their product, and not just managers who spend their time improving the process.

Do not get me wrong, process is important, but our leadership team members know that product trumps process. If I have a leadership team member who spends more time on process than product, it is my job to mentor them, so they become a stronger leader. So, I continually emphasize the importance of the product over the process, so my leadership team members never lose sight of our main job and so they do not fall into the manager's black hole.

As I have mentioned, knowing your product requires a leader to know their numbers, but it is not always as simple as that. Sometimes, gut instinct is needed, as well. I recently attended a student orientation organized by one of our program chairs to greet students on behalf of the faculty and staff in our school. I was invited to give a welcome address and to give our students a word of encouragement.

During the event, I noticed all program faculty were up front as a group except for one faculty member. To me this was a bit concerning. They were a team; why would this one faculty member not feel part of the team? I asked my Associate Dean to *'look under the hood.'* Was something going on that we needed to address?

Similarly, this past year I saw faculty members meeting regularly in one of the faculty offices. This is not usually a concern, but their faces told me that the conversations were difficult. After one of these meetings, I talked to the chair of the department and asked, "*I have noticed some of your faculty members meeting often behind closed doors. Is there something going on that we should know about?*"

In both situations, there were things going on, but my leadership team members were able to bring the issues to the surface and deal with them, and we were able to make our school and our faculty team stronger because we had the courage to focus on our *'product'* and to take the time to *'look under the hood.'*

Chapter 7 – Lessons Learned

Although all organizational leaders need to be both managers and leaders, if you want to become a leader, you must spend more time *'leading'* than *'managing.'*

To become an effective leader must develop a *'leader-first'* mindset. A leader-first mindset is one in which a leader views their primary role not as a manager, but as a leader.

One of the best methods of learning about your organization and getting things done is for a leader to use the *Leading By Wandering Around* (LBWA) leadership practice.

As a leader it is important to focus your time on knowing and improving the *'product'* of your organization rather than focusing only the *'processes'* used to develop your product.

Chapter 8

Final Thoughts

In most organizations, the term '*bottom line*' is most often used when referring to the profitability of the organization. In higher education, the bottom line is tuition revenue, which is driven by student enrollment and retention.

As a Dean, I have always paid attention to our school's bottom line and no one has ever had to tell me how well we were doing well, because I review our enrollment numbers and revenue numbers. When I became the Dean of the Liffrig Family School of Education and Behavioral Sciences in 2010, we had 15 full-time faculty, 325 undergraduate students in seven undergraduate programs, 150 graduate students in three graduate programs, generated 10,000 undergraduate credits and 3,000 graduate credits

During the next 10 years, we added numerous academic programs at both the undergraduate and graduate levels and started four undergraduate online programs, as well. We also created new organizational charts with additional academic program administrators, including two new chair positions, namely, Chair of Graduate Counseling and Chair of Undergraduate and Graduate Social Work.

However, the major change was the addition of faculty who were strong leaders, administrators and classroom instructors who believed in our mission. I actively participated in the hiring of every faculty member in our school with all our current full-time faculty hired during my tenure. Our faculty and our leadership team members have intentionally focused on hiring the right faculty for every faculty position in our school. When I refer to the right faculty, I am referring to faculty who believe in who we are as an institution and as a school. Faculty who are team players who thought more about our students and our programs than themselves. We tried to hire faculty who we believed would thrive in our *dynamic* organizational culture.

About five years ago, at a higher education conference I attended, I participated in a Deans' Roundtable discussion on current issues deans face in this higher education environment. During the roundtable discussion, I was challenged by another dean on my leadership decision to try to hire people based on mission and who were a good fit for our school. I mentioned to this dean that I assumed she was thinking that in doing so, I was primarily looking for faculty who looked like me and who had similar backgrounds and experiences.

Although she did not respond to my comment, I let her know this was not the case at all. In fact, I told her the faculty I have hired have been primarily women and that my current Associate Dean was a Hispanic and Native American woman who not only did not look like me but thought about things differently than I usually did. I also mentioned I had hired a Psychology faculty member who was a woman from India and who happened to be Hindu. I indicated that these two faculty members were not only great hires, but they were great faculty who helped us build our *dynamic* organizational culture because they were extremely competent faculty members who also believed in who we were as an institution and a school.

I think people, like the dean who questioned me about our hiring process, thought I believed in hiring only like-minded people to build our strong organizational culture when the opposite is true. Having people with different thoughts and ideas is crucial if you want to build a strong *dynamic* organizational culture. However, you need people who believe in the organization and who think more about what is good for the organization instead of what is best for them.

We have made hiring mistakes, and I have had to make the difficult decision of letting faculty go, but with those few exceptions, we have made good hiring decisions. The faculty we have hired have helped build our school and helped us create a place where great people want to work.

It has taken us over 10 years to get to where we are today. Our school's academic programs and the number of faculty in our school hired for these programs have increased significantly. Currently, we have 29 full-time faculty who teach over 600 undergraduate students in 13 undergraduate programs and 350 graduate students in 9 graduate programs. Our school generates over 15,000 undergraduate credits and over 5,400 graduate credits, and we have had a 47% increase in our undergraduate net revenue and a 120% increase in our graduate net revenue.

In addition, another bottom-line marker that supports building a *dynamic* organizational culture is faculty and staff retention. Since the Covid-19 Pandemic, most organizations in America have been suffering from what is being called the *'Great Resignation'* in which record numbers of employees have decided voluntarily to quit their jobs. Employee retention has become a significant human resources problem and higher education is not immune from this problem.

In an article in The Higher Education Chronical, Megan Zahneis analyzed the data from the CUPA-HR's Higher-Education Employee Retention Survey and found that, *"...retention problems that have plagued higher ed for years show no sign of subsiding...".*

Her analysis of the data found that, *"While pay was the top cause of dissatisfaction reported by survey respondents, other, more nuanced forms of discontent also emerged. Nearly a quarter of employees said they didn't feel they were recognized for their contributions, while about 40 percent didn't feel they could bring up problems or tough issues at work, or that they belonged".*

Our school has been able to maintain a high faculty and staff retention rate with a faculty turnover rate that is lower than the 2022-23 national reported turnover rate of 14.3% and a staff turnover rate that is much lower than the 15.2%

turnover rate. Although I cannot provide empirical evidence that our low faculty and staff turnover rate is due to the creation of our school's *dynamic* organizational culture, it is one of the variables that has helped us retain our faculty and staff.

Our leadership team members and I have given personal attention to building our *dynamic* organizational culture, and not given it just lip service. We work each day to make our *dynamic* organizational culture stronger and each day focus our energies on taking the steps needed to help our culture thrive and grow.

My guess is that very few organizational leaders would argue with me about the need for and importance of a strong, *dynamic* organizational culture, but few I believe truly know where to begin when trying to create or build it. I have worked for leaders who did not have a good understanding of how to build a *dynamic* organizational culture and, as a result, it never became a primary focus but only a secondary concern. These leaders failed to realize the power of an organization's culture and, therefore, spent little time actively trying to build it. Instead, they focused their time on those things they could manage and measure. Unfortunately, an organization's culture is like the air we breathe - it is hard to see and touch, but no organization can thrive without it.

Due to an organizational leader's lack of knowledge on how to create and build their organization's *dynamic* culture, most leaders try to emulate the cultures of other effective organizations rather than taking the time to learn how to create their organization's own *dynamic* culture. I saw this firsthand as a college basketball coach. If a well-known coach from an NCAA Division I ran a certain offense or defense that was successful, you were sure to see other coaches emulating that style, regardless of their talent or their team's makeup.

Unfortunately, organizations, just like sports' teams are uniquely different with each organization having members with different talents and skills. In addition, each organization has its own unique product, processes and mission and vision. The challenge for each organizational leader is learning how to develop and create their organization's own *dynamic* organizational culture rather than trying to emulate another similar organization.

In a recent online article in *Working Knowledge* from the Harvard Business School, James Heskett reviewed research from Duke University that found 76 percent of executives in business organizations believe they have not done as much as they could to improve their organization's culture, with executives often reluctant to try to take on such a challenge.

Based on his research, Heskett believes that organizational leaders are likely discouraged from taking on the task of building and changing their own organization's culture, because it is perceived to be too complex, chances of success are low, and simply takes too long. Heskett states:

"The question fostering the widest range of opinions among those whose counsel I value is ... just how long it takes to change a culture. Among many, there is a perception that organizational culture change takes a long time, longer than the tenure of a leader, longer than the attention span of the organization—so long that other high-priority initiatives by necessity will distract the organization from completing the effort."

I think Heskett is right; most organizational leaders give up trying to change their organization's culture because they believe it is too time-consuming, complex, difficult, and, therefore, a fruitless effort. But without strong leaders who genuinely believe in the value of building a *dynamic* organizational culture, it will never happen.

As Heskett states, *"Studies have shown that the single most important element in determining success in changing an organization's culture is the interest, support, and even passion displayed by its leader."*

So, if you are a leader of any organization, if you genuinely believe in the value of spending your time on building culture and believe an organization's culture is important, then the time you spend on building your organization's culture will not be time wasted. Building an organizational *dynamic* culture is not easy and does not happen overnight, but it is well worth the effort and is often the major reason a leader and/or organization either fails or succeeds.

The reason I chose to write this book is because I believe in the power of a *dynamic* organizational culture, and I want leaders to understand that building their organization's culture is not only a leader's most important responsibility but the one thing that will determine a leader's success. In today's world, an organization's culture cannot remain static; it must be a *dynamic* organizational culture that inspires innovation and creativity.

Every organization today is in a highly competitive business climate and if the leader in that organization wants the organization to succeed, they must create a *dynamic* organizational culture that is adaptable and receptive to change, where striving to do better and focusing on the thinking and learning necessary for continuous improvement is the norm.

The building of our school's *dynamic* organizational **TEAM** culture has taken a tremendous amount of time, work and required sacrifices. Initially, I personally spent 50 to 60 hours a week and sleepless nights trying to make it all come to fruition. I believed in what we were doing, but it took time before we reaped the benefits of our work and got faculty buy-in.

The number one thing I did for our school was to believe in what we were trying to build and to spend my time building our *dynamic* organizational culture. I must admit that I spent the first few years, as Dean, struggling to find the time to lead, because I was immersed in simply just finding the time to get things done. My time was focused on improving processes and doing tasks. I was clearly more of a manager than a leader because there was so much to do.

Initially, I plugged along with the help of other faculty members, trying to build our *dynamic* culture one day at a time, but as we built our leadership team, things slowly came together. The journey has been worth it and only now, a decade later, have we begun to reap the benefits of our labor.

So, my final thought for all leaders is to define what you want your organization to become, develop a leader-leader mindset, create a leadership team, define your leadership team's leadership principles, create an organization where every member of the organization has been given the responsibility and authority to help the organization perform effectively and try your best to focus on leading, instead of managing. It will be a challenging journey but well worth it.

Afterword

People will say, *"He's a born leader."* But true leadership is not innate. Rather, the humanistic dynamics of true leadership stem from prioritizing opportunities, deeply understanding emotional intelligence, enthusiastically embracing intentional listening, and, most importantly...allowing oneself to be vulnerable in pursuit of organizational trust. Collectively, each of these characteristics contributes to great leadership. The key often lies in the extent to which an individual reflects upon where one stands in the continuum toward profound leadership in each of these four areas.

If you were to ask Dr. Jonas where he is today regarding his leadership skills, he would likely offer he is still building toward his own perceived notion of strong leadership. In fact, he may add he has never quit honing his skills and seeks to further understand human nature in all its complexities in order to '*lift*' his junior colleagues toward their unique measure of professional competency in leading others. True leaders are not in it for themselves; and they are in it for the organization. In the words of Dr. Jonas, *"I am building a TEAM here!"*

Over a career that has spanned decades, Dr. Jonas has learned (sometimes in ways that would make some leaders in the same situation shrink in angst) how to find solutions to difficult organizational problems and, better yet. He has a real commitment to sharing his hard-earned expertise with other aspiring leaders in the hope of perpetuating a team spirit and organizational culture, which includes daring to take chances.

Strong leaders are always searching for the next opportunity to further the organization...to develop the team. Often, the structure in which this type of momentum can be fostered is via a keen sense of duty and personal commitment. Everyone in the organization must be personally responsible for something. When you lead an organization in which everyone recognizes their own personal stake in the outcome, it creates autonomy that can withstand external economic, social, and/or political environmental fluctuations. These external pressures may present challenges in the day-to-day operational function of the team; however, the strength of the team will not be crushed by these forces. The reasons behind this perseverance are attributed to how the talents and strengths of each member of the team contribute to the overall success of the organization.

On more than one occasion, rather than hire an individual who only minimally met the expectations of the Jonas TEAM at the University of Mary, the search would instead continue for another semester or even academic year. In the meantime, the TEAM picked up courses, workloads, and administrative responsibilities until the right hire was made. A direct reflection of the much-lauded quote by Theordore Roosevelt:

"The best leader is the one who has sense enough to pick good men to get what he wants done, and self-restraint enough to keep from meddling with them while they do it."

'Waiting out' a great hire is notably a luxury not afforded to all organizations, and certainly not in today's K-12 environment, where classrooms are filled with young learners while the administrator (leader) of that building is looking at few to no applications for that position—in August! So, while the philosophy hailed by Roosevelt and practiced by Dr. Jonas seems in the best interests of the overall organization, I concede the application may not be a perfect fit in all cases.

One of the most taxing sets of leadership skills to master is reflexive emotional intelligence. From my perspective, it is deeply hinged by generational differences. As a "boomer," my worldview is quite different than our younger generation of leaders. Dr. Jonas is of the same demographic, and we often reflected on how we could better understand the emotional and intellectual needs of our young leaders. What seems so second nature from our desk is not…by a long shot from theirs. I became better at it in some measure and will jokingly say...he is still working on it! Yet the point being that the future of leadership with respect to moving an organization forward really depends on this critical skill. Work-life balance is not a myth. It exists and is paramount in understanding young leadership in today's workforce. It drives their decisions and perpetuates itself within the work environment in the daily interactions among colleagues. A lack of emotional intelligence in addressing this important leadership element could result in a fractured workforce that looks like 'us and them' rather than a team.

In keeping with Roosevelt's idea of self-restraint, perhaps this is most aligned with the art of intentional listening. Our basic human nature begs us to offer our opinion...to weigh in. The temptation is particularly acute in situations where listening is the ***most needed*** leadership strategy to address a critical organizational situation. A mirage of things hinders true listening, primarily ego and an 'agenda' that solicits a mental solution to a problem before it is fully described because you (the leader) perceive to already know the solution! A recent paper published by the Harvard Business Review (2021) suggested modern leaders consider this acronym to address the temptation of not intentionally listening: WAIT, which translates into "Why am I Talking?" To be great in leadership, you must be willing to remain fully present and listen. Otherwise, you run the risk of not finding the best solution to the problem because all you can see is your own solution. In the world of Dr. Jonas, the administration TEAM was trained discretely in this art each month as we hashed out all that was occurring in our different departments, waiting upon the listening ears present in the room to offer perspectives, which would ultimately bring forth solutions or perhaps interventions. We worked on this month after month, year after year. It became part of what the administration TEAM did to fulfill the expectations of the faculty and staff, who we were all responsible for serving through our leadership.

Finally, the influence of vulnerability and trust in the role of leadership. To me, vulnerability is like taking your *'leadership pulse.'* Are you able to weather the potential for the challenge from your team? Can you navigate the discussion where your initiatives may be met with criticism, and, even more important…will your colleagues feel they have a place at the table to bring their concerns/dissonance forward? Which renders: Is there trust in your workplace environment? Being vulnerable does not mean you have a target on you waiting for the next dagger instead, it looks more like walking into the office of a colleague and simply talking—about anything, noticing how your colleagues and junior leaders are interacting daily—the banter and laughter among your TEAM members, calling a 'cabinet meeting' at the local bistro at 4:30 on a Thursday afternoon—just because, and witnessing your leadership team come together simply to bounce ideas off each other and seek support. When your organization operates in this way, you have built trust. Dr. Jonas has said many times, "We are not a family here. We are a TEAM." The nuance is that you do not choose who your family members are, nor are you able to be rid of them! However, each TEAM member has been carefully chosen for their talent and skill to work in unison toward the mission and vision of the organization.

I am grateful for the opportunity I have been given to work with Dr. Jonas. Our connection regarding the future of the Liffrig Family School of Education and Behavioral Sciences was mutually supportive. Over the years, we have shared many life stories and sometimes tears over things that have brought us to where we are at the University of Mary today. His heart is that of a leader who cares deeply about his organization and everyone who has been brought into the school to support our students. He is a great human being, and I am deeply honored to call him my colleague and friend.

Carmelita Lamb, Ph.D., Professor, Associate Dean, University of Mary (retired)

Acknowledgments

As I near retirement and reflect on my years of service in education and at the University of Mary, I am humbled by the blessings I have been given and different career opportunities I have had in my life and the family that has supported me during my entire professional career. Growing up in a small rural town in southeastern Minnesota provided me with meaningful experiences that taught me the value of hard work and the importance of family and community, but with few worldly experiences that challenged my belief system.

Thankfully, I had parents who believed in me and a dad who tried his best to provide me with the opportunities to pursue my desire to play college basketball. I grew up at a time when there were limited opportunities to practice playing basketball. The high school gym closed after 6 pm when the custodian went home, and there were no other basketball facilities in our town. So, my dad and I took an old piece of plywood, bolted a basketball rim to it and set it up in one of the Quonset buildings at the grain elevator in town that he managed. He gave me a set of keys for the building and said, *"Now you have your basketball court."*

I remember the first night I went to play basketball in the Quonset building with my basketball friends, and the basketball court that day I created was full of pallets of seed and feed bags with no room to practice. Together we tried to remove the bags, but after an hour or so, we realized it was going to take forever. So, I went to the office just inside the building and called my dad. My dad answered the phone, and I said, *"Dad, there are pallets of seed and feed in the way, so we cannot play basketball."* He replied, *"Well, that's too bad and hung up."*

We went back to moving bags when I heard a forklift start-up at the end of the Quonset building. I looked up and saw my dad on the forklift, and in minutes, he moved the feed and seed bags. As he was leaving, I said, *"Dad. Why didn't you come earlier to help us remove the bags."* He responded with, *"I wanted to know how bad you wanted to play."*

At that moment, my dad taught me a great lesson, which was if you want something in life, you need to make the decision to put your heart into it and pursue it with passion. I took that first lesson with me on my leadership journey, and it has served me well. Thank you, dad.

As I moved from the world of basketball as a player and coach into higher education administration and various leadership roles, I took the same passion I had for basketball with me into my new role as an organizational leader. I tried my best to lead from my heart with a commitment to serve those under my care. In addition, I tried to find others who could lead alongside me who had a similar drive and desire to build something special. Fortunately, I found those people, and I am forever grateful for their willingness to join them on my journey.

In 2009, I was hired by the University of Mary President, Monsignor James Shea, as the first Dean of the Liffrig Family School of Education and Behavioral Sciences. Although I believed I possessed the leadership skills needed to be a dean, I realized at the time that Monsignor Shea was taking a gamble on hiring me as a dean. I had little experience in higher education administration except as the Chair of the Department of Education at the University of Mary. I had spent the first 25 years of my career chasing my dream of being a successful basketball coach, so I had limited experiences as a higher education administrator. Yet, he must have seen something in me that made him believe I could do the job. I will be forever grateful to him for giving me this opportunity and realize how fortunate I was to be in a dean position. Since the first day I became a Dean, I have tried my best not to let him or the university down.

Throughout my career, my closest teammate has been my wife, Shirley, who has been at my side throughout my entire career. She has always given me support and allowed me time away from home to follow my passion as a coach and as an organizational leader. Sir Ernest Shackleton penned the following leadership quote, "*Leadership is a fine thing, but it has its penalties. And the greatest penalty is loneliness.*"

Without someone by a leader's side supporting them, the leadership burden can be overwhelming for leaders. Fortunately for me, my wife has been there during the tough times and has helped me stay focused, grounded and believing in myself.

At the University of Mary, I have worked alongside incredibly talented, dedicated and committed faculty and staff. These people have been the primary reason for my success as a dean and are the reason I have chosen to stay at the University of Mary for the past 35 years. I have been fortunate to hire faculty and staff who believed in what we were trying to accomplish and who saw their position not as a job but as a vocation. They have truly been the major reason for our school's success, and it has been a joy to collaborate with them in building our *dynamic* school culture.

Our faculty are committed to our students, each other and believe in the mission of the University of Mary. For any leader who wants to succeed, I suggest putting your time and energy into finding and hiring competent people who are great teammates and who will bring out the best in others. As a leader, you can be the most competent and talented leader on earth, but you cannot do it alone. As Ray Kroc, the founder of McDonald's, was quoted as saying, "*You are only as good as the people you hire.*"

Thank you, University of Mary, and thank you to everyone who chose to become a faculty or staff member in our school. Every one of you is a special person with unique gifts, and you have brought so much joy into my life and the students you serve. I will never forget you and thank you for making the decision to become a member of the University of Mary community and for becoming a member of our **TEAM**.

References – Chapter 1

Aldridge, J., & Fraser, B. (2017). Teachers' perceptions of the organizational climate: A tool for promoting instructional improvement. *School Leadership & Management, 38*(3), 323–344.

Alfonso, R. (1986). *The unseen supervisor: Organization and culture as determinants of teacher behavior.* Presentation at Annual Meeting of the American Educational Research Association (67th), San Francisco, CA.

Atiles, J. T. (2017). Values and beliefs regarding discipline practices: How school culture impacts teacher responses to student misbehavior. *Educational Research Quarterly, 40*(3).

Balthazard, P. A., Cooke, R. A., & Potter, R. E. (2006). Dysfunctional culture, dysfunctional organization: Capturing the behavioral norms that form organizational culture and drive performance. *Journal of Managerial Psychology, 21,* 709–732.

Beaudoin, M.H. & Taylor, M. (2004). *Creating a positive school culture: How principals and teachers can solve problems together.* Corwin Press, Sage Publications Co., Thousand Oaks, CA.

Bektas, F., Çogaltay, N., Karadag, E. & Ay, Y. (2015) School culture and academic achievement of students: A meta-analysis study, *The Anthropologist, 21*(3), 482-488.

Berberoglu, A. (2018). Impact of organizational climate on organizational commitment and perceived organizational performance: empirical evidence from public hospitals. *BMC Health Services Research, 18*(1).

Buckingham, M. (2011). Stand Out as a Leader. *Leadership Excellence, 28*(10), 17.

Burkus, D. (2014, December 2). *How to tell if your company has a creative culture.* Harvard Business Review.

Cotenoff, Scott (2019, April 2). *Building a Dynamic Organizational Culture: It Takes More than Leaders.* La Piana Consulting (Blog).

Davis, J. R., & Warner, N. (2015). Schools matter: The positive relationship between New York city high schools' student academic progress and school climate. *Urban Education, 53*(8), 959–980.

Deal T. E. & Kennedy, A. A. (2000) *Corporate cultures: The rites and rituals of corporate life.* Cambridge, MA: Perseus Books.

Drucker, P. F. (1977). *People and performance: The best of Peter Drucker on management.* New York: Harper's College Press.

Ehrhart, M. G., Schneider, B., & Macey, W. H. (2014). *Organizational Climate and Culture* (1st ed.). Bingdon, Oxfordshire, United Kingdom: Routledge.

El-Amin, Z. N., (2017). *The relationship between positive behavior interventions and supports and school climate/culture in elementary schools.* (67) [Master's Thesis, Louisiana Tech University].

Emihovich, C., & Battaglia, C. (2000). Creating cultures for collaborative inquiry: New challenges for school leaders. *International Journal of Leadership in Education, 3*(3), 225-238.

Engels, N., Hotton, G., Devos, G., Bouckenooghe, D., & Aelterman, A. (2008). Principals in schools with a positive school culture. *Educational Studies, 34*(3), 159–174.

Ferren, A. S., Kennan, W. R., & Lerch, S. H. (2001). Reconciling corporate and academic cultures. *Peer Review*, 3, Spring.

Gaziel, H.H. (1997). Impact of school culture on effectiveness of secondary schools with disadvantaged students. *Journal of Educational Research, 90,* 310-318.

Goodman, E. A., Zammuto, R. F., & Gifford, B. D. (2001). The competing values framework: Understanding the impact of organizational culture on the quality of work life. *Organization Development Journal, 19*, 58 – 68.

Gregory, B. T., Shook, C. L., Armenakis, A. A., & Harris, S. G. (2009). Organizational culture and effectiveness: A study of values, attitudes, and organizational outcomes. *Journal of Business Research, 62*(7), 673–679.

Gruenert, S. (2000). Shaping a new school culture. *Contemporary Education, 2*(71), 14-17.

Gruenert, S., & Whitaker, T. (2019). *Committing to the culture: How leaders can create and sustain positive schools.* Alexandria: ASCD.

Hargreaves, D. H. (1995). School culture, school effectiveness and school improvement. *School Effectiveness and School Improvement, 6*, 23-46.

Kohm, B., & Nance, B. (2009). Creating Collaborative Culture. *Educational Leadership, 67*(2), 67-72.

Le Clear, E. A. (2005). *Relationships among leadership styles, school culture, and student achievement* [Unpublished doctoral dissertation]. The University of Florida.

Lee, S. K. J., & Yu, K. (2004). Corporate culture and organizational performance. *Journal of Managerial Psychology, 19*, 340 –359.

Levin, D. Z., Cross, R., Abrams, L. C., & Lesser, E. L. (2003*).* Trust and knowledge sharing: A critical combination. In Lesser, E. (Ed.) *Creating value with knowledge: Insights from the IBM Institute for business value* (36-41). Cary, NC: Oxford University Press.

Lok, P., & Crawford, J. (2004). The effect of organizational culture and leadership style on job satisfaction and organizational commitment: A cross-national comparison. *Journal of Management Development, 23*, 321–338.

MacNeil, A. J., Prater, D. L. Prater & Busch, S. (2009). The effects of school culture and climate on student achievement. *International Journal of Leadership in Education, 12*(1), 73-84.

MacTavish, M. D., & Kolb, J. A. (2008). *An Examination of the Dynamics of Organizational Culture and Values-Based Leader Identities and Behaviors: One Company's Experience.* [Paper presentation] Academy of Human Resource Development International Research Conference in the Americas: Panama City, FL.

Maslowski, R. (2001). *School culture and school performance.* Twente, the Netherlands: Twente University Press.

Mees, G. W. (2008). *The relationships among principal leadership, school culture, and student achievement in Missouri middle schools.* [Unpublished doctoral dissertation]. University of Missouri – Columbia.

Millerd, P. (2019, November 1). *Edgar Schein - organizational culture: Artifacts, values & assumptions.* Paul Millerd.

Nahavandi, A., Denhardt, R. B., Denhardt, J. V., & Aristigueta, M. P. (2015). *Organizational behavior* (1st ed.). SAGE Publishing.

National Center for Education Statistics. (2023). *Immediate College Enrollment Rate. Condition of Education.* U.S. Department of Education, Institute of Education Sciences.

O'Reilly, C. A. (1989). Corporations, culture, and commitment: Motivation and social control in organizations. *California Management Review, 31*, 9 –25.

O'Reilly, C. A., & Chatman, J. A. (1996). Culture as social control: Corporations, cults and commitment. *Research in Organizational Behavior, 18*, 157–200.

O'Reilly, C. A., Chatman, J. A., & Caldwell, D. M. (1991). People and organizational culture: A profile comparison approach to assessing person– organization fit. *The Academy of Management Journal, 34*, 487–516.

Owens, R. G., & Valesky, T. C. (2015). *Organizational behavior in education: leadership and school reform.* Prentice Hall.

Peters, T. J., & Waterman, R. H. Jr. (1982). *In search of excellence: Lessons from America's best companies.* Harper & Row, New York, NY.

Piotrowsky, M. J. (2016). *The impact of leadership on school culture and student achievement.* (1623) [Dissertation, Clemson University].

Queen, L. (2017, July 13). *Artifacts: A powerful driver of your organization's culture.* Colloquia Partners. Retrieved February 23, 2023.

Sanchez, J. E., Paul, J. M., & Thornton, B. W. (2020). Relationships among teachers' perceptions of principal leadership and teachers' perceptions of school climate in the high school setting. *International Journal of Leadership in Education*, 1–21.

Schafer, L. (2018, July 23). *What makes a good school culture?.* Harvard Graduate School of Education.

Schafer, L. (2018, September 09). *Building a strong school culture.* Harvard Graduate School of Education.

Schein, E. H. (2017). *Organizational culture and leadership* (5th ed.). John Wiley & Sons, Inc., Hoboken, New Jersey.

Shrm. (2021, June 3). *Understanding and Developing Organizational Culture.* SHRM. Taras, V., Kirkman, B. L., & Steel, P. (2010). Examining the impact of culture's consequences: A three-decade, multi-analytic review of Hofstede's cultural dimensions. *Journal of Applied Psychology, 95*, 405–439.

Urick, A., & Bowers, A. J. (2011). What influences principals' perceptions of academic climate? A nationally representative study of the direct effects of perception on climate. *Leadership and Policy in Schools*, *10*(3), 322–348.

Vislocky, K. (2005), *The relationship between school culture and student achievement in middle schools.* (631) [Dissertation, University of Central Florida].

VerBurg, S. (2019, May 30). *How to Get a Leadership Mindset.* Dale Carnegie of Orange County.

Voight, A., Austin, G., and Hanson, T. (2013). A climate for academic success: How school climate distinguishes schools that are beating the achievement odds (ED559741). ERIC.

Warrick, D. D. (2017). What leaders need to know about organizational culture. *Business Horizons*, *60*(3), 395–404.

Wong, K. (2020, May 7). *Organizational Culture: Definition, Importance, and Development.* Engage Blog.

References – Chapter 2

Bass, B. M. (1985). Leadership and Performance Beyond Expectations. New York: Free Press.

Bass, B. M., & Avolio, B. J. (1994). *Transformational leadership: Improving organizational effectiveness.* Thousand Oaks, CA: SAGE.

Bass, B. M., & Riggio, R. E. (2014). *Transformational leadership.* Routledge.

Bennis, W. G. (2009). *On becoming a leader* (4th ed.). Basic Books.

Blane, H. (2017). *7 principles of transformational leadership: Create a mindset of passion, innovation, and growth.* Career Press.

Bonnici, C. A. (2011). *Creating a Successful Leadership Style: Principles of Personal Strategic Planning.* Rowman & Littlefield Education.

Brigadier General (Ret.) Becky Halstead and Brigadier General (Ret.) Maureen LeBoeuf, & (USA, B. G. B. H. (2021, February 26). *Creating, Sharing and Living a Leader Philosophy.* ChiefExecutive.net.

Bryant, S.E. (2003). The role of transformational and transactional leadership in creating, sharing and exploiting organizational knowledge. *Journal of Leadership and Organizational Studies*, 9(4), pp. 32-44.

Burns, J.M. (1978) *Leadership.* New York. Harper &Row Burkus, D. (2020, December 18). *Transformational Leadership Theory.*

Dobbs, R., & Walker, P. R. (2010). *Transformational leadership: a blueprint for real organizational change.* Parkhurst Brothers, Inc.

Duyan, M., & Yildiz, S. M. (2020). The Effect of Transformational Leadership on Job Satisfaction: An

Investigation on Academic Staffs at Faculties of Sports Sciences in Turkey. *Online Submission*, 7(2), 364–373.

Francisco, C. D. C. (2019). School Principals' Transformational Leadership Styles and Their Effects on Teachers' Self-Efficacy. *Online Submission*, 7(10), 622–635.

Judge, T.A. & Piccolo, R.F. (2004). Transformational and transactional leadership: A meta-analytic test of their relative validity. *Journal of Applied Psychology*, 89/5, pp. 755-768.

Kark, R., Shamir, B., & Chen, G. (2003). The two faces of transformational leadership: Empowerment and dependency. *Journal of Applied Psychology*, 88, 246-255.

Kark, R., Van Dijk, D., & Vashdi, D. R. (2018). Motivated or Demotivated to Be Creative: The Role of Self-Regulatory Focus in Transformational and Transactional Leadership Processes. *Applied Psychology: An International Review*, 67(1), 186–224.

Krzyzewski, Mike & Phillips, D.T. (2000). *Leading with the Heart: Coach K's Successful Strategies for Basketball, Business, and Life.* Warner Books, Inc., New York, NY.

Maccoby, M. (2014, August 1). *Why People Follow the Leader: The Power of Transference.* Harvard Business Review.

Marquet, L. D. (2019). *Turn the ship around!: A true story of turning followers into leaders.* Portfolio.

Masterson, M. (2017). Building the Right Culture for the Organization. *FBI Law Enforcement Bulletin*, 7–9.

McKee, A., Boyatzis, R. E., & Johnston, F. (2008). *Becoming a resonant leader: Develop your emotional intelligence, renew your relationships, and sustain your effectiveness.* Harvard Business Press.

Nahavandi, A., Denhardt, R. B., Denhardt, J. V., & Aristigueta, M. P. (2015). *Organizational behavior* (1st ed.). SAGE Publishing.

Odumeru, J. A., & Ogbonna, I. G. (2013). Transformational vs. Transactional Leadership Theories: Evidence in Literature. *International Review of Management and Business Research, 2*(2).

Riggio, R. E. (n.d.). *The 4 Elements of Transformational Leaders*. Psychology Today.

Rijal, S. (2010). Leadership style and organizational culture in a learning organization: A comparative study. *International Journal of Management & Information Systems (IJMIS), 14*(5).

Ruvolo, C. M., Peterson, S. A., & LeBoeuf, J. N. G. (2004). Leaders Are Made, Not Born The Critical Role of a Developmental Framework to Facilitate an Organizational Culture of Development. *Consulting Psychology Journal: Practice and Research, 56*(1), 10–19.

Sarros, J. C., Gray, J., & Densten, I. L. (2002). Leadership and its impact on culture. *International Journal of Business Studies, 10*(1), 1–26.

Serin, H., & Akkaya, A. (2020). The Relationship between School Principals' Perceived Transformational Leadership Behavior and Teachers' Motivation. *International Education Studies, 13*(10), 70–87.

Shinagel, M. (2021, March 12). *The Paradox of Leadership - Professional Development: Harvard DCE*. Professional Development | Harvard DCE.

Tourish, D. (2013). The Dark Side of Transformational Leadership: A Critical Perspective. *Development and Learning in Organizations: An International Journal, 28*(1).

Van Dijk, D., Kark, R., Matta, F., & Johnson, R. E. (2021). Collective aspirations: Collective regulatory focus as a mediator between transformational and transactional leadership and team creativity. *Journal of Business & Psychology, 36*(4), 633–658.

Walumbwa, F. O., Avolio, B. J., & Zhu, W. (2008). How transformational leadership leaves its influence on individual job performance: The role of identification and efficacy beliefs. *Personnel Psychology*, 61, 793-825.

Walumbwa, F. O., & Hartnell, C. A. (2011). Understanding transformational leadership–employee performance links: The role of relational identification and self-efficacy. *Journal of Occupational and Organizational Psychology*, 84(1), 153-172.

Warrick, D. D. (2017). What leaders need to know about organizational culture. *Business Horizons*, 60(3), 395–404.

Warrick, D. D., & Gardner, D. G. (2021). Leaders Build Cultures: Action Steps for Leaders to Build Successful Organizational Cultures. *Journal of Leadership, Accountability & Ethics*, 18(1), 36–52.

References – Chapter 3

Balkundi, P., & Harrison, D. A. (2006). Ties, leaders, and time in teams: Strong inference about network structure's effects on team viability and performance. *Academy of Management Journal, 49*, 49-68.

Bennis, W. G. (2009). *On becoming a leader*. Basic Books.

Brass, D. J. (2012). *A social network perspective on organizational psychology*. In S. W. J. Kozlowski (Ed.), The Oxford Handbook of Organizational Psychology. New York: Oxford University Press.

Buskens, V. W. (2002). *Social networks and trust*. Hingham, MA: Kluwer Academic Publishers.

Carmeli, A. (2005). The relationship between organizational culture and withdrawal intentions and behaviour. *International Journal of Manpower, 26*, 177–195.

Capano, C. (2019, September 30). *Council Post: Five Basic Principles Of Highly Effective Leadership*. Forbes.

Coleman, James S. (1988). Social capital in the creation of human capital. *American Journal of Sociology, 94*. Supplement S95-S120.

Collins, J. C. (2009). *Good to great: why some companies make the leap... and others don't*. Collins.

Cross, R., Baker, W., & Parker, Andrew. (2003). What creates energy in organizations? *MIT Sloan Management Review, 45*, 51-56.

Craig, W. (2019, May 7). *8 Team Leadership Principles For Project Success*. Forbes.

Cross, R., & Prusak, L. (2002). The people who make organizations go—or stop. *Harvard Business Review, 80*, 105-112.

Duhigg, C. (2016, February 25). *What google learned from its quest to build the perfect team.* The New York Times.

Goodall, A. (2023). *Credible: The power of expert leaders.* BASIC BOOKS.

Hitch, C. (2017, July 20). *Creating a culture of trust in organizations.* Ideas for Leaders.

Horsager, D. (2012). *The Trust Edge: How Top Leaders GainFaster Results, Deeper Relationships.* Free Press.

Hunter, G. S. (2016). *Small acts of leadership: 12 intentional behaviors that lead to big impact.* Bibliomotion, Inc.

Kohm, B., & Nance, B. (2009). Creating Collaborative Culture. *Educational Leadership, 67*(2), 67-72.

Kouzes, J. M., & Posner, B. Z. (2017). *The leadership challenge: how to make extraordinary things happen in organizations.* The Leadership Challenge.

Lencioni, P. (2012). *The advantage: Why organizational health trumps everything else in business.* Jossey-Bass.

Lencioni, P. (2018). *The ideal team player: How to recognize and cultivate the three essential virtues: A leadership fable.* Wiley India.

Lencioni, P., & Stransky, C. (2002). *The Five Dysfunctions of a Team.* Random House, Inc.

Manick, C. J. D. (2016). *Knowing better: Improving collective decision making in higher education shared governance* [ProQuest LLC].

Marquet, L. D. (2019). *Turn the ship around!: A true story of turning followers into leaders.* Portfolio.

NDSU Magazine: ESPN Gameday. North Dakota State University. (n.d.).

Parris, M. A. (2003). Work teams: Perceptions of a ready-made support system?. *Employee Responsibilities and Rights Journal, 15*, 71– 83.

Rousseau, V., Aube´, C., Chiocchio, F., Boudrias, J.-S., & Morin, E. M. (2008). Social interactions at work and psychological health: The role of leader–member exchange and work group integration. *Journal of Applied Social Psychology, 38*, 1755–1777.

Schmidt, E. & Rosenberg, J. (2014). *How google works*. New York, NY: Grand Central from the perspective of an administrator. *Education, 126*(4), 763-768.

Sinek, S. (September 10, 2018). *What it means to lead, or: go forth and do well*. ArkLaTex Chapter of the Armed Forces Communications and Electronics Association.

Sinek, S. (2019). *Start with why: how great leaders inspire everyone to take action*. Penguin Business.

Sinek, S. (2019). *Leaders eat last: why some teams pull together and others don't*. Penguin Business.

Sinek, S. (2020). *The Infinite Game*. London, England: Portfolio Penguin.

YouTube. (2014, June 23). *Teamwork - The Steve Jobs 1985 Macintosh Computer Team (2)*. YouTube.

Whitaker, R (1972). *Dealing with difficult teachers* (2nd ed.). Larchmont, NY: Eye on Education.

Willink, J., & Babin, L. (2018). *The dichotomy of leadership: balancing the challenges of extreme ownership to lead and win*. St. Martin's Press.

Willink, J., & Babin, L. (2018). *Extreme ownership: How U.S. navy seals lead and win*. Macmillan.

References – Chapter 4

Axelrod, A. (2012). *Julius Caesar, CEO: 6 principles to guide & inspire modern leaders*. Sterling.

Baloglu, N. (2012). Relations between Value-Based Leadership and Distributed Leadership: A Causal Research on School Principles' Behaviors. *Educational Sciences: Theory and Practice, 12*(2), 1375–1378.

Behar, H. (200&). *It's Not About the Coffee: Leadership Principles from a Life at Starbucks*. Portfolio.

Brearley, B. (2021, July 9). *Why Leaders Don't Delegate Tasks (and How to Fix It)*. Thoughtful Leader.

Caldwell, C. (2017). Lakota virtues and leadership principles: insights and applications for ethical leaders. *Journal of Management Development, 36*(3), 309–318.

Davidson, S., & Butcher, J. (2019). Rural Superintendents' Experiences with Empowerment and Alignment to Vision in the Application of Principle-Centered Leadership. *Rural Educator, 40*(1), 63–72.

Denning, Stephen (2007). *The Secret Language of Leadership: How Leaders Inspire Action Through Narrative*. San Francisco: Jossey-Bass.

Gaskell, A. (2021, March 23). *Why People Don't Always Speak Up At Work*. Forbes. Graf, K. (2019).

Graf, Katie (2019). Understanding Principles of Sustainable Leadership: An Examination of Stress Factors Which Challenge Urban High School Principals [ProQuest LLC]. In *ProQuest LLC*.

Hargreaves, A., & Fink, D. (2004). The Seven Principles of Sustainable Leadership. *Educational Leadership, 61*(7), 8.

Heckelman, W. (2017). Five Critical Principles to Guide Organizational Change. *OD Practitioner, 49*(4), 13–21.

Hedlund, W. (2019, January 19). *9 Reasons Leaders Don't Delegate*. Transforming Leader.

Logan, R. J. (2004). Leadership Lessons from the Marines: 11 Leadership Principles, Adapted from U.S. Marines Training, Provide a Useful Guide for School Administrators. *Principal*, *84*(2), 47–49.

Manby, J. (2012). *Love Works: Seven Timeless Principles for Effective Leaders*. Zondervan, Grand Rapids, MI.

Martineau, P. (2012). Principles of Good Principals: Effective Leadership Brings a Board's Vision to the School Level. *Education Digest: Essential Readings Condensed for Quick Review*, *77*(8), 53–58.

McKee, A., Boyatzis, R. E., & Johnston, F. (2008). *Becoming a resonant leader: develop your emotional intelligence, renew your relationships, and sustain your effectiveness*. Harvard Business Press.

Moyers, E. L. (2000). Principles of Leadership. *Executive Excellence*, *17*(12), 11.

Sheehan, N. T., & Isaac, G. E. (2014). Principles operationalize corporate values so they matter. *Strategy & Leadership*, *42*(3), 23–30.

Sherf, E. N., Parke, M. R., & Isaakyan, S. (2021). Distinguishing Voice and Silence at Work: Unique Relationships with Perceived Impact, Psychological Safety, and Burnout. *Academy of Management Journal*, *64*(1), 114–148.

Strelecky, John P. (2008). *The Big Five for Life: Leadership's Greatest Secrets: A Story of One Man and Leadership's Greatest Secret*. Little Brown Book Group.

Walton, B. (2008). Making Sense of Leadership: Exploring the Five Key Roles Used by Effective Leaders/On Leadership: Essential Principles for Success. *Library Journal*, *133*(16), 81.

Welch, J. (2015, October 27). *Drive Business Growth by Building the Right Team*. YouTube.

YouTube. (2021, July 13). *USA Women's Olympic VOLLEYBALL Documentary | 2020 One | Episode 1*. YouTube.

References – Chapter 5

Akhtar, N., & Hassan, S. S. (2021). Conflict Management Styles as Predictors of Organizational Commitment in University Teachers. *Journal of Behavioural Sciences, 31*(1), 98–123.

Akin, U. (2021). Exploring the Relationship between Emotional Labor and Organizational Commitment Levels of Teachers. *Eurasian Journal of Educational Research, 91*, 61–82.

Anand, V., Joshi, M., & O'Leary-Kelly, A. M. (2013). An organizational identity approach to strategic groups. *Organization Science, 24*(2), 571–590.

Ashforth, B. E., Harrison, S. H., & Corley, K. G. (2008). Identification in organizations: An examination of four fundamental questions. *Journal of Management, 34*, 325-374.

Ateş, A., & Ünal, A. (2021). The Relationship between Diversity Management, Job Satisfaction and Organizational Commitment in Teachers: A Mediating Role of Perceived Organizational Support. *Educational Sciences: Theory & Practice, 21*(1), 18–32.

Benedictine Sisters of Annunciation Monastery. Annunciation Monastery. (2021).

Brewer, M., & Gardner, W. (1996). What is this "We"? Levels of collective identity and self-representation. *Journal of Personality and Social Psychology*, 71(1), 83-93.

Brickson, S. L. (2012). Athletes, best friends, and social activists: An integrative model accounting for the role of identity in organizational identification. *Organization Science.*

Brown, A. D., & Humphreys, M. (2006). Organizational identity and place: A discursive exploration of hegemony and resistance. *Journal of Management Studies, 43*, 231-257.

Brown, A. D., & Starkey, K. (2000). Organizational identity and organizational learning: A psychodynamic approach. Academy of Management Review, 25, 102-120.

Carmeli, A., Atwater, L., & Levi, A. (2011). How leadership enhances employees' knowledge sharing: The intervening roles of relational and organizational identification. *Journal of Technology Transfer*, 36, 257-274.

CBS Interactive. (2017, May 7). *How the Chicago Cubs finally won the World Series after 108 years*. CBS News.

Chickering, A. W., and L. Reisser. 1993. *Education and identity*. San Francisco: Jossey-Bass.

Cooper, D., & Thatcher, S. M. B. (2010). Identification in organizations: The role of self-concept orientations and identification motives. *Academy of Management Review*, 35, 516-538.

Corley, K. G., & Gioia, D. A. (2004). Identity ambiguity and change in the wake of a corporate spin-off. *Administrative Science Quarterly*, 49, 173-208.

Corley, K. G., Harquail, C. V., Pratt, M. G., Glynn, M. A., Fiol, M., & Hatch, M. J. (2006). Guiding organizational identity through aged adolescence. *Journal of Management Inquiry*, 15, 85-99.

Corley, K.G. (2004). Defined by our strategy or our culture? Hierarchical differences in perceptions of organizational identity and change. *Human Relations*, 57:1145-1177.

Coyle, D. (2018). *The culture code: the secrets of highly successful groups*. Bantam.

Dale, K., & Fox, M. L. (2008). Leadership style and organizational commitment: the mediating effect of role stress. *Journal of Managerial Issues*, 20(1).

Diamond, M. A. (2017). *Discovering organizational identity: Dynamics of relational attachment*. University of Missouri Press.

Dutton, J. E., Dukerich, J. M., & Harquail, C. V. (1994). Organizational images and member identification. *Administrative Science Quarterly*, 39, 239-263.

Dvorak, N., & Ott, B. (2021, May 13). *An Organization's Identity Has to Inspire Customers*. Gallup.com.

Edwards, M. R., & Peccei, R. (2010). Perceived organizational support, organizational identification, and employee outcomes. *Journal of Personnel Psychology*, 9(1), 17-26.

Ellemers, N., De Gilder, D., & Haslam, S. A. (2004). Motivating individuals and groups at work: A social identity perspective on leadership and group performance. *Academy of Management Review*, 29, 459-478.

Fiol, M.C. (2002). Capitalizing on a paradox: The role of language in transforming organizational identities. *Organizational Science*, 13:653-666.

Fiorito, J., Bozeman, D. P., Young, A., & Meurs, J. A. (2017). Organizational commitment, human resource practices, and organizational characteristics. *Journal of Managerial Issues*, *19*(2).

Gibney, R., Zagenczyk, T.J., Fuller, J.B., Hester, K. & Caner, T. (2011). Exploring organizational obstruction and the expanded model of organizational identification. *Journal of Applied Social Psychology*, 41, 1083-1109.

Gioia, D.A., Price, K.N., Hamilton, A.L. & Thomas, J.B. (2010). Forging an identity: An insider-outsider study of processes involved in the formation of organizational identity. *Administration Science Quarterly*, 55:1-46

Habib, H. (2020). Organizational Commitment among Secondary School Teachers in Relation to Job Burnout. *Shanlax International Journal of Education*, *8*(3), 72–76.

Hatch, M. J., & Schultz, M. (2002). The dynamics of Organizational Identity. *Human Relations*, 55(8), 989–1018.

Harquail, C. V., & King, A. W. (2010). Construing organizational identity: The role of embodied cognition. *Organization Studies*, 31, 1619-1648.

Harrison, J. D. (2000). Multiple imaginings of institutional identity. *Journal of Applied Behavioral Science*, 36, 425-455.

Hatch, M. J., & Schultz, M. (2011). *Organizational identity: a reader*. Oxford University Press.

Henry, T. (2018). *Herding Tigers: be the leader that creative people need*. Portfolio.

Hsu, G., & Elsbach, K. D. (2013). Explaining variation in organizational identity categorization. *Organization Science*, *24*(4).

Kenny, K., Whittle, A., & Willmott, H. (2011). *Understanding identity & organizations*. SAGE.

Kjaergaard, A., Morsing, M., & Ravasi, D. (2011). Mediating identity: A study of media influence on organizational identity construction in a celebrity firm. *Journal of Management Studies,* 48, 514-543.

Kreiner, G. E., & Ashforth, B. E. (2004). Evidence toward an expanded model of organizational identification. *Journal of Organizational Behavior*, 25(1), 1-28.

Lerpold, L. (2008). *Organizational identity in practice*. Routledge.

Pasha, S., & Aftab, M. J. (2020). The Effect of Job Involvement, Organizational Commitment, and Job Satisfaction on Turnover Intention. *Information and Knowledge Management*, *23*(2).

Mahajan, A., Bishop, J. W., & Scott, D. (2012). Does trust in top management mediate top management communication, employee involvement and organizational commitment relationships? *Journal of Managerial Issues*, *22*(4).

Prati, L. M., McMillan-Capehart, A., & Karriker, J. H. (2009). Affecting organizational identity: A manager's influence. *Journal of Leadership & Organizational Studies*, 15(4), 404–415.

Ran, B., & Duimering, P. R. (2007). Imaging the organization: Language use in organizational identity claims. *Journal of Business and technical Communication*, 21, 155-187.

Ravasi, D. & Schultz, M. (2006). Responding to organizational identity threats: Exploring the role of organizational culture. *The Academy of Management Journal*, 49:433-458.

Riantoputra, C. D. (2010). Know thyself: Examining factors that influence the activation of organizational identity concepts in top managers' minds. *Group and Organization Management*, 35, 8-38.

Riketta, M. (2005). Organizational identification: A meta-analysis. *Journal of Vocational Behavior*, 66:358-384.

Seppala, E., & King, M. (2021, August 27). *Burnout at work isn't just About Exhaustion. It's also about loneliness.* Harvard Business Review.

Schultz, M., & Hernes, T. (2013). A Temporal Perspective on Organizational Identity. *Organization Science*, *24*(1), 1–21.

Scott, S.G., & Lane, V. R. (2000). A stakeholder approach to organizational identity. *Academy of Management Review*, 25, 43-62.

Smith, E. B. (2011). Identities as lenses: How organizational identity affects audiences' evaluation of organizational performance. *Administrative Science Quarterly*, 56, 61-94.

Stensaker, B. (2014). Organizational identity as a concept for understanding university dynamics. *Higher Education*, *69*(1), 103–115.

Ucar, R., & Dalgic, S. (2021). Relationship between School Principals' Strategic Leadership Characteristics and School

Teachers' Organizational Commitment Levels. *Eurasian Journal of Educational Research, 91*, 105–126.

Voss, Z. G., Cable, D. M., & Voss, G. B. (2006). Organizational Identity and Firm Performance: What Happens When Leaders Disagree About "Who We Are?" *Organization Science, 17*(6), 741–755.

Vough, H. (2012). Not all identifications are created equal: Exploring employee accounts for workgroup, organizational, and professional identification. *Organization Science*, 23, 778-800.

Walumbwa, F. O., Mayer, D. M., Wang, P., Wang, H., Workman, K., & Christensen, A. L. (2011). Linking ethical leadership to employee performance: The roles of leader-member exchange, self-efficacy, and organizational identification. *Organizational Behavior and Human Decision Processes,* 115(2), 204-213.

Willmott, H., Whittle, A., & Kenny, K. (2011). *Studying identity & organizations.* Sage.

Workplace Culture Institute, LLC. (2021, January 5). *Organizational identity.* Sheila Margolis.

Yi, X., & Uen, J. F. (2006). Relationship between organizational socialization and organization identification of professionals: Moderating effects of personal work experience and growth need strength. *Journal of American Academy of Business*, 10(1), 362-371.

YouTube. (2019, May 17). *The Simple Secret To Happiness | Ryan Estis Inspirational Video| Goalcast.* YouTube.

References – Chapter 6

Andrade, M. S. (2016). Effective Organizational Structures and Processes: Addressing Issues of Change. *New Directions for Higher Education, 2016*(173), 31–42.

Argote, L., Ingram, P., Levine, J. M., & Moreland, R. L. (2000). Knowledge transfer in organizations: Learning from the experience of others. *Organizational Behavior and Human Decision Processes, 82*(1), 1–8.

Balkundi, P., & Harrison, D. A. (2006). Ties, leaders, and time in teams: Strong inference about network structure's effects on team viability and performance. *Academy of Management Journal, 49*, 49-68.

Bambra, C., Egan, M., Thomas, S., Petticrew, M., & Whitehead, M. (2007). The psychosocial and health effects of workplace reorganisation: A systematic review of task restructuring interventions. *Journal of Epidemiology and Community Health, 61*, 1028 – 1037.

Burke, W. (2014). *Organization change: Theory and practice* (4th ed.). Thousand Oaks, Calif.: Sage Publications.

Cummings, J. N., & Cross, R. (2003). Structural properties of work groups and their consequences for performance. *Social Networks, 25,* 197-210.

Dumay, X. (2009). Origins and consequences of schools' organizational. *Educational Administration Quarterly, 45* (4), 523–555.

Durham, S., Merritt, J., & Sorrell, J. (2007). Implementing a new faculty workload formula. *Nursing Education Perspectives (National League for Nursing), 28*(4), 184–189.

Emihovich, C., & Battaglia, C. (2000). Creating cultures for collaborative inquiry: New challenges for school leaders. *International Journal of Leadership in Education, 3*(3), 225-238.

Gayle D. J., Tewarie B., White A. Q. Jr. (2003). *Governance in the twenty-first-century university: Approaches to effective leadership and strategic management.* Hoboken, NJ: John Wiley.

Griffith, A. S., & Altinay, Z. (2020). A framework to assess higher education faculty workload in U.S. universities. *Innovations in Education & Teaching International, 57*(6), 691–700.

Hagedorn, L. S. (2000). Conceptualizing faculty job satisfaction: Components, theories and outcomes. *New Directions for Institutional Research, 105*, 5-20.

Hass, M. (2020, April 18). Shared Governance Is a Strength During the COVID-19 Crisis (opinion). *Inside Higher Ed.*

Ingram, D. (2019, March 12). *Why is organizational structure important?* Small Business - Chron.com.

Kater, S. T. (2017). Community college faculty conceptualizations of shared governance: Shared understandings of a sociopolitical reality. *Community College Review, 45*(3), 234–257.

Keeling, R. P., Underhile, R., & Wall, A. F. (2007). Horizontal and vertical structures: The dynamics of organization in higher education. *Liberal Education, 93*(4), 22-31.

Kezar, A. (2009). Change in higher education: Not enough or too much? *Change: The Magazine of Higher Learning, 41.* 18-23.

Kezar, A., & Lester, J. (2009a). *Organizing higher education for collaboration.* San Francisco: Jossey-Bass.

Kezar, A. (2020, April 13). *Why the top-down governance structures of higher education need revitalizing.* USC Rossier School of Education.

Kohm, B., & Nance, B. (2009). Creating Collaborative Culture. *Educational Leadership, 67*(2), 67-72.

Krylova, K. O., Vera, D., & Crossan, M. (2016). Knowledge transfer in knowledge-Intensive organizations: The crucial role of improvisation in transferring and protecting knowledge. *Journal of Knowledge Management, 20*(5), 1045–1064.

Lambert E. G., Qureshi H., Klahm C., Smith B., Frank J. (2017). The effects of perceptions of organizational structure on job involvement, job satisfaction, and organizational commitment among Indian police officers. *International Journal of Offender Therapy and Comparative Criminology, 61*(16). 1892-1911.

Levin, D. Z., Cross, R., Abrams, L. C., & Lesser, E. L. (2003*). Trust and knowledge sharing: A critical combination.* In Lesser, E. (Ed.) *Creating value with knowledge: Insights from the IBM institute for business value* (36-41). Cary, NC: Oxford University Press.

Longin, T. C. (2002). *Institutional governance: A call for collaborative decision making in American higher education.* In McMillen, L. A., & Berber, J. (Eds.), A new academic compact: Revisioning the relationship between faculty and their institutions. (pp. 211- 221). Bolton, MA: Anker.

Mahmoudsalehi, M., Moradkhannejad, R. & Safari, K. (2012). How knowledge management is affected by organizational structure, *The Learning Organization,* (19)6, 518-528.

Martínez-León, I. M. & Martínez-García, J. A. (2011). The influence of organizational structure on organizational learning, *International Journal of Manpower, 32*(5/6), 537 – 566.

Mintzberg, H. (1979). *The structuring of organizations: A synthesis of the research.* Englewood Cliffs, NJ: Prentice-Hall.

Mitchell, B. (2023, May 18). *Council post: The road to better governance in American Higher Education.* Forbes.

Nahavandi, A., Denhardt, R. B., Denhardt, J. V., & Aristigueta, M. P. (2015). *Organizational behavior* (1st ed.). SAGE Publishing.

Olson, G. A. (2020, July 23). *Exactly What Is 'Shared Governance'?* The Chronicle of Higher Education.

Ransom, S., Hinings, B., & Greenwood, R. (1980). The structuring of organizational structures. *Administrative Science Quarterly, 25*, 1-17.

Schmidt, E. & Rosenberg, J. (2014). *How google works.* New York, NY: Grand Central

Simplicio, Joseph S. C. (2006). Shared governance: An analysis of power on the modern university campus from the perspective of an administrator. *Education, 126*(4), 763-768.

Tierney W. G. (2004). *Competing conceptions of academic governance.* Baltimore, MD: Johns Hopkins University Press.

Weick, K. E. (1976). Educational organizations as loosely coupled systems.

References – Chapter 7

Akbar, A. (2013). How to differentiate between 'Leadership' and 'Management' Function in Organization: A Review of Scholarly Thoughts. *International Journal of Economics Business and Management Studies*, 2(1), 38–44.

Algahtani, A. (2014). Are leadership and management different? A review. *Journal of Management Policies and Practices*, 2(3), 71–82.

Arruda, W. (2021, April 2). *9 Differences Between Being A Leader And A Manager*. Forbes.

Buhler, P. (1995). Leaders vs. managers. *Supervision*, 56(5), 24.

Buss, D. (2001). When Managing Isn't Enough: Nine Ways to Develop the Leaders You Need. (Cover story). *Workforce (10928332)*, 80(12), 44.

Gentry, W. A., Griggs, T. L., Deal, J. J., Mondore, S. P., & Cox, B. D. (2011). A comparison of generational differences in endorsement of leadership practices with actual leadership skill level. *Consulting Psychology Journal: Practice and Research*, 63(1), 39–49.

Godin, P. (1998). Achieving Vision: Managers vs. Leaders. *Manage*, 50(1), 10.

Guttmann, R. C. (1994). Leaders and managers: Dimensions and differences. *People & Education*, 2(2), 135.

Nayar, V. (2014, August 7). *Three differences between managers and leaders*. Harvard Business Review.

Katzman, C. N. (1999). Differences between leaders and managers. *Modern Healthcare*, 29(40), 53.

Kotter, J. P. (2012). *Leading change*. Harvard Business Review Press.

Managers vs. leaders. (1977). *Management Review*, 66(8), 60.

McKendrick, J. (2020, April 6). *Is 'management by walking around' still possible when everything is digital and remote?* Forbes.

Melin, H. (2021, February 22). *How to think like a leader, not a manager: 3 ways to build a culture of trust.* Adobe Workfront.

Pozin, I. (2016, March 22). *How to Be a Leader, Not a Manager.* Inc.com.

Prussakov, G. (2009, May 12). *20 differences between Management & Leadership.* Affiliate Marketing Blog by Geno Prussakov.

Reynolds, J. G., & Warfield, W. H. (2010). Discerning the Differences Between Managers and Leaders. *Education Digest, 75*(7), 61–64.

Serrat, O. (2017). *Knowledge solutions: Tools, methods, and approaches to drive organizational performance.* Springer.

Sinek, S. (2019, October 23). *Simon Sinek: Leader versus manager.* YouTube.

Valiga, T. M. (2019). Leaders, managers, and followers: Working in harmony. *Nursing, 49*(1), 45–48.

Villanova University. (2020, January 16). *How to Be a True Leader and a Better Manager.* villanovau.com.

Voigt, B., & Guariglia, J. (2015). Managers vs. Leaders. *Leadership Excellence, 32*(10), 14–15.

Ward, M. (2020, September 18). *17 of the biggest differences between managers and leaders.* Business Insider.

White, H. S. (1990). Managers and Leaders: Are There More Differences Than Similarities? *Library Journal, 115*(11), 51–53.

References – Chapter 8

Bichsel, Jacqueline; Fuesting, Melissa; Schneider, Jennifer; & Tubbs, Diana. (2022, July). *The CUPA-HR 2022 Higher Education Employee Retention Survey: Initial Results*. CUPA-HR.

Gorysberg, B., Lee, J., Price, J., & Cheng, J. Y.-J. (2022, December 15). *The Leader's Guide to Corporate Culture*. Harvard Business Review.

Graham, J. R., Harvey, C. R., & Rajgopal, S. (2021). Corporate culture: Evidence from the field. *SSRN Electronic Journal*.

Heskett, J. (2021, November 1). *How long does it take to improve an organization's culture?* HBS Working Knowledge.

Schein, E. H. (2017). *Organizational culture and leadership* (5th ed.). John Wiley & Sons, Inc., Hoboken, New Jersey.

Zahneis, M. (2023, September 14). *Higher Ed's Work-Force-Retention Problems Aren't Going Away*. https://www.chronicle.com/article/higher-eds-work-force-retention-problems-arent-going-away.

Made in the USA
Las Vegas, NV
03 March 2025

2a4eaf8c-7fb9-4216-aa24-508a356925b5R01